HOLLYWOOD BOOK REVIEWS

A Capitol Idea

by Bill Hause

Hollywood Book
EXCELLENT MERIT
Reviews

HOLLYWOOD
Book Reviews

book review by David Allen

BOOKWRIGHTS
HOUSE

There is so much to praise in this book. Not only is it a hair-raising ride through a kingdom of political woe; it is also a cautionary tale for our time.

—David Allen
Hollywood Book Reviews

A Capitol Idea

BY BILL HAUSE

Some folks out there are spreading the malicious rumor that literary fiction dead. Not true. A Capitol Idea, a novel by Bill Hause, puts that notion to re decisively. It is rare to come upon a novel that is so bristling with brio, charr manic humor and — timeliness. Meeting the crazies and their oh so crazy wor in Hause's fiction would be, I imagine, something akin to waking up in the ear 18th century and cracking open a brand-new edition of Gulliver's Travels...tha how crazy, variegated and ultimately caricaturing the denizens of A Capitol Ide really are.

In a somewhat mythic dystopia — more than faintly evocative of our own tim right down to the names and specific politics and issues under fire – a mo unlikely antihero, Sean Fidwitter aka King Sean I, aka Sean the Commoner, Sean the Benevolent, proclaims Ebony Rock ("Isla de Granita de Ebano") th new homeland for the homeless impoverished and neglected peoples of th world. The road to Hell is paved with good intentions: imagine the three rir circus of grief and catastrophe this announcement then creates!

steeplechase of corrupt self-promoters, politicians, lawyers and consultants escend upon the scene, eager to squirrel away their portion. Me Me Me...you now the drill. Isla de Granita de Ebano may just as well be Greenland, or Mars: ne allusions in this book to current political events are spot on and uncanny. (In ne book, Isla de Granita may be, for example, the next hot source of lithium, or ven diamonds. See what I mean? The analogy to space exploration is key ere.) Lieutenant Colonel Karl Helmut Wolfgang von Schvinghammer, lexandre Begré (idealistic attorney for human rights), and A. Gunner-Ellis rafty political pretender), are just a few of the very eccentrically named and ery memorable characters making an outright spectacle of themselves in this asted landscape of competing egos and ecological ruin.

nere is so much to praise in this book. Not only is it a hair-raising ride through kingdom of political woe; it is also a cautionary tale for our time. The rotagonists and creeps and bad guys in this roiling madcap novel are mirrors eld up to our society and up to our ever-scrambling selves. In their desperate achinations to turn a profit, to grab power, it is easy to trace the author's take n today's headlines: Trump, Musk, Greenland, Mars, all the rest...I suspect the ook was written quickly, in response to recent political events, but it sure is a owerful write, a most rousing one.

few words on the structure and cadence of this book. Hause is clearly a fan nd student of 18th century novels. His book shares some of the rollicking ensibility you see in amazingly funny books from that time like Tristam Shandy. ot just that, but the author brackets the text with topical headers and aptions, really like one would see in the works of Victorian and earlier authors.

es, Bill Hause writes from the shoulders of giants, giants of comedy novels like Confederacy of Dunces and The Sot-Weed Factor. Hause taps into this living erary tradition and succeeds in making it ever fresh. A Capitol Idea, Bill ause's take on America 2.0, is a fast-moving morality play/novel that leaves e reader breathless, as do the bounteous associations, historical allusions nd rich language of the narrative. Hause is an amazing storyteller for our time.

ll Hause's writing encourages readers to reflect on the delicate balance etween benevolent intentions and the pervasive influence of corruption, aking it a noteworthy addition to contemporary literature.

HOLLYWOOD
Book Reviews

A CAPITOL IDEA
The Early Daze

A Political Thriller

BILL HAUSE

978-1-965552-53-7 (Paperback)
978-1-965552-52-0 (Hardback)

BOOKWRIGHTS
HOUSE

admin@bookwrightshouse.com
☎ (213) 286 6700

Dedication

To Myra, Robert, and Linda

Acknowledgements

I WISH TO CONVEY MY most profound appreciation and gratitude to my hometown friends and proofreaders, my former neighbor and pre-reviewer Charles "Chuck Wilder," and my onetime high school theatrical "leading lady," creative *muse* and dramatic adviser, Diana Holcomb Ruhl without whose assistance and encouragement, the writing of this book might never have been completed.

Table of Contents

Preview

"IF AN ISLAND LAND mass larger than Greenland that mysteriously emerges on the equator from the depths of the Atlantic Ocean isn't enough to capture your interest and imagination, then consider what may happen when circumstances turn this "private island" into the sole property of one Sean Fidwitter, a commoner with royal connections.

Fidwitter, an irresponsible, aimless but convivial *"Bon Vivant"* with a healthy sense of humor and compassion for the world's poor and downtrodden, enlists the help of an old college friend, Alexandre Begre', now a renowned international lawyer. As Begre' forms an illustrious team to bring to fruition Sean's dream of making his island sub-continent a haven and home for the homeless and indigent. A powerful Triad of opposition to Sean's plans quickly set themselves to work implementing their own schemes for this new land of opportunity, but the island holds its own secrets which bring their own dynamic into play.

Thus, <u>A Capitol Idea</u> - Book One - "The Early Daze", by author Bill Hause, lays the "groundwork" for an expedition of discovery not only of the new island but of social and political issues and systems that resonate with our times."

—Chuck Wilder.

PROLOGUE

"Our Mother is Dying"

———◇———

"The Great Spirit is in all things. He is in the air we breathe. The Great Spirit is our Father, but the Earth is our mother. She nourishes us…That which we put into the ground she returns to us."

> —Big Thunder Wabanaki, Algonquin

"Treat the earth well: it was not given to you by your parents, it was loaned to you by your children. We do not inherit the Earth from our Ancestors; we borrow it from our Children."

> —Ancient Indian (Indigenous Peoples, Native American) Proverb.

"We must protect the forests for our children, grandchildren, and children yet to be born. We must protect the forests for those who can't speak for themselves such as the birds, animals, fish, and trees." Qwatsinas

> —(Hereditary Chief Edward Moody), Nuxalk Nation.

THE UNIVERSE IS AN infinite, violent realm in ever-expanding chaos, birth, growth, maturity, and death; bright, twinkling, distant and faint stars, clusters and binaries, Solar, Hot Blue, Red Dwarf and Red Giant Stars, White Dwarfs, Neutron Stars, and Black Holes.

Planet mae karen pie s, whether hostile or friendly to emerging, sustainable living organisms, are formed from particles of gas and dust. They collide and fuse with interstellar debris, asteroids, meteors, fireballs, icy comets, and sometimes minor planets while orbiting a star. The heavier, rocky planets form nearest to the star, their gases blown away by solar winds, their positions within the elliptical orbits of the solar system determined by the gravity of their star and the larger gaseous planets.

The rocky planet Earth in the Milky Way galaxy was miraculously, fatefully, or randomly located precisely in the right place of its solar system, possessing protective atmospheric compositions of nitrogen, oxygen, and argon, (gaseous and liquid), an abundance of surface water, borrowed or stolen from other rocky planets and asteroids, orbiting at a safe distance from its light and heat emitting star for the birth, development, and sustenance and viability of life.

"Mother Earth is vomiting toxic waste."
—Author.

Commencing primarily during the Industrial Revolution, humankind had been dumping its waste upon the Earth, burying its poisons in the soil, polluting the sky, and contaminating its rivers, lakes, oceans, and waterways. The only inhabitable planet within its solar system in the Milky Way galaxy had become one massive landfill.

The frequency of volcanic eruptions, earthquakes, hurricanes, tornadoes, heat waves, droughts, flash floods, and blizzards caused another misanthropic doomsday observer to declare, "We have made our planet terminally ill. We poisoned it. It is vomiting millions of years of toxic waste.

"Our Mother Earth Is Dying, And We Are All Complicit in Her Murder."

—Author.

Increasingly, across the spectrum, various groups of individuals both within and out of the science community spoke of relocating people to Mars, the moons of Jupiter or Saturn, or to inhabitable exoplanets millions of light years from Earth.

Devout environmentalists bluntly shamed the lazy, science-denying planet trashers with their poor history, placing profits above responsible land stewardship and labeling them as complacent cowards, ever reminding them, "It is the responsibility of those who made the mess to clean it up!"

Large corporations tasked with multi-million-dollar clean-up costs.

"Recycling, land and water reclamation, and these environmental regulations are not cost-effective and far too labor-intensive!"

Argued the corporate and individual abusers as they constantly fought ecological civil lawsuits.

The corporate accountants observed, "It may be cheaper in the long run to abandon this spaceship and allow it to heal naturally."

The Earth was a hostile planet at war with itself, embroiled in an unending struggle between climate change advocates and science deniers, economic class disparities, irreconcilable political division, demagoguery, heated conspiracies, racial conflicts, xenophobia, misogyny, and culture wars.

Chapter One

"IN THE DOLDRUMS"

—◇—

"If a man knows not to which port he
sails, no wind is favorable."

—Seneca.

"You weren't thinking, and you weren't
paying attention either. People who don't
pay attention often get stuck in the
Doldrums."

—Norton Juster.

NEW ATLANTICA WAS IN the doldrums, where nothing
ever happens and only meteorologists and
climatologists take notice of its weather.
Sailing vessels in the long-ago Age of
Discovery drifted aimlessly in still waters,
floundering in the calm, still, windless
waters along this equatorial belt, its captain
and crew pleading in final desperation to
a distant, deaf deity for delivery. The
captain was angered at his navigator, and
the ship's overworked surgeon was annoyed
by having their card game interrupted by
the inexperienced shanghaied hostage crew
and New World-bound seasick passengers

hanging over the deck railings, returning the rotten fish and spoiled crab dinner to the sea that produced it. With no lush land sightings from the crow's nest, the crew scanned the cloudless skies in vain for a miraculous sudden burst of strong winds or even a seasonal rainstorm to thrust them from peril, feverish sightings of seaworthy ships gliding effortlessly across God-forsaken still waters independent of sails. Abandoned by all mankind and facing slow agonizing death from starvation and thirst in an ocean of inedible sea life and non-potable salt water, the captain and officers face armed mutinies of frightened and desperate men unwilling to die at sea and looking for someone to blame for their cruel demise. Eventually, navigators and cartographers gained wisdom from seafaring disasters by altering the shipping routes around the doldrums, placing the windless ocean deserts between the shipping routes throughout the age of discovery, well into the modern age of ocean liners, naval cruisers, troop ships, and nuclear battleships and submarines.

Those seafaring voyagers who miraculously escaped the windless, still waters of the doldrums returned with warnings to either avoid the convergence zones entirely or to minimize sailing time there by quickly crossing it at its narrowest point, avoiding seasonal cyclones and thunderstorms.

For hundreds of thousands of eons, long before the dawning of another millennium on the eve of the changing of the Century

Guard, it lay unobtrusively, uncharted, and unknown near the ocean floor, balancing perilously upon a jagged and eroding subterranean mountain shelf. Over time, the underwater sub-continent escaped the grip of the decaying shelf through natural erosion and drifted upward toward the surface, surfacing above the equator, in a tedious glacier-like movement sustained by the swirling underwater currents and torrential tidal storms.

However, when this newest and now largest of the planet's islands; the main island alone encompassing over 2330990 sq. km. (900,000 sq. mi.), 800,000 miles in length from its most southernmost tip to its northern jutting into the treacherous Darwin Straits and 100,000 miles in width from its rugged west coast to its jagged and mountainous east coast finally surfaced, it received only cursory notice and limited fanfare as the global community of nations and countries was already far too consumed with their own fragile socio-political and economic trade alliances and petty rivalries to show any interest in the discovery of an inconsequential equatorial land mass.

The Seasonal trade island winds met at the Intertropical Convergence Zone (ITCZ) as the doldrums narrowed, producing intense thunderstorms and torrential rainstorms that drenched the main island until it was blanketed with vast green forests and grasslands that produced surprisingly abundant vegetation. A natural, luscious green canopy shaded the rich soil. It camouflaged the only indigenous creatures, the Aquarians, the Ybanies, and other cryptids, from seasonal shifts of the ITCZ toward and away from the equator that produced long, intensely wet and dry seasons.

The expansive lush green main island was home to aquatic animals and mammals, tide pools of star fish, anemones and sponges, snails, sea turtles, sea lions barking on rocks and hungry sharks in the ocean, dark forests, rocky ridges and thick vegetation, hominids and maybe even fabled humanoids, the Aquarians possessing the mystical but undocumented with any solid scientific evidence to change shape and disappear into the rocks and foliage.

New Atlantica originally was meant to designate the entire archipelago. Still, future pretentious residents call the main island with its thick vegetation, forests, and foliage as Greatsylvania to distinguish it from the small Perimeter Islands (and hundreds of asteroid belt-like islets) that formed an impenetrable boundary around the self-important main island; rendering any future development of commercial ports-of-call. The black granite, boulder-like island across the Darwin Straits from the northern tip of the main island was eventually named Granito de Ebano as a place reserved by Greatsylvanian snobs and elitists for the great unwashed and the culturally undesirables; the socially unredeemable boorish, boisterous, and

4

crude menial laborers, recalcitrant petty criminals, the habitually impoverished, the uneducated and perpetually relapsing drug and alcohol addicts. In general, all those denizens who were to be denied any reasonable and equitable opportunity to rise and compete for a higher rung in society's ladder of success.

Thus, New Atlantica was to be left to its own devices in its early daze to succeed or fail miserably gloriously; prosper or perish; to feast or famine or to lead or follow; to stumble in humans, stagnate or progress or collapse from perpetual exhaustion and fall into the inertia of oblivion.

Chapter Two

"I CAN SEE GRANITO DE EBANO FROM HERE..."

⚜

"The mining industry might make wealth and power for a few men and women, but the many would always be smashed and battered beneath its giant treads."

—Katharine Susannah Prichard.

"My own view is that this planet is used as a penal colony, lunatic asylum and dumping ground by a superior civilization (sic), to get rid of the undesirable and unfit. I can't prove it, but you can't disprove it either."

—Christopher Hitchens.

ISLA DE GRANITO DE Ebano (SP. Island of Ebony Granite), across the Darwin Straits from New Atlantica's northernmost, needle-nosed point before the mass immigration to the main island, was and more conveniently for non-Spanish speakers called "the black boulder." In time, it would be revealed that it encompassed much more than a slick and slippery black granite boulder, a small island jutting skyward from the swirling eddies in treacherous, unnavigable Darwin Straits. This rocky island, 5,456 square miles (14,130.98 sq. km) in area, approximating the size of a small country, colony, or the State of Connecticut in the United States, was inhabited by inmates, deportees, and others ostracized by society, cultures, and communities. All but completely ignored and neglected by New Atlantica's earliest settlers, the elitist, exclusionary leading islanders, Granito de Ebano was formed even prior to the settlement of the main island by *the Mongrels* strictly as a mining colony, The *Granito De Ebano Rock Mining Company* by the J.J.(Jake) Gillis Enterprises to segregate and isolate The Great Unwashed; boorish, boisterous, and crude menial laborers, recalcitrant criminals, the habitually impoverished, the uneducated and unpolished, drug and alcohol addicts and all those deemed by main island status quo devoid of any redeemable social value. Under constant surveillance by military security drones, the Granito de Ebanos lived under *"virtual Dickensian workhouse arrest,"* beneath the yoke of poverty, strict draconian control, and scrutiny without any of the most basic freedoms and liberties; speech, voting, labor negotiations, freedom of movement and any of the most basic autonomous of human rights including population control, religion, and political activism. They were, for all intents and purposes, worker bees pejoratively known as moles.

In general, all those denizens were prevented from any reasonable and equitable rise and competition to the higher rungs on the proverbial ladder of success. A series of colonial governors, whose salaries, inflated fees, and exaggerated allowances were regularly misappropriated through these workers' payroll deductions, administered the day-to-day management, maintaining a safe distance from Isla de Granito de Ebano. The governor and staff's spacious and lavish residential compound sat securely across the straits on the northern tip of the main island, where the workers' toils and activities were under constant surveillance by the most intricate and detailed vigilance of military satellites and sophisticated listening devices. The governor and staff rapidly evaded threats of capture as hostage bargaining pawns by accessing the two private 18-passenger jets with vital classified documents, equipment, and luggage aboard the helicopters at the small airport within his gated compound. As the governor *quipped*, "I can see Isla de Granito de Ebano quite safely from here and even that's too damn close."

Chapter Three

IN THE BEGINNING, THERE WERE THE AQUARIANS

⊰⊱

"Men are beastly and natural, and when touched by God, the One who is supernatural, they become as 'mythical creatures'—only more true and just, and therefore all the meeker."

—Criss Jami.

"The scariest monsters are the ones that lurk within our souls."

—Edgar Allan Poe

THE AQUARIANS, SELDOM SIGHTED by any human unless by drug induced hallucinations, complete fabrications and hoaxes, or sheer imagination were the island's first inhabitants, its natives, and indigenous beings; mysterious, mystical chameleon-like, shape-altering (through mass hypnosis and telekinesis) indigenous humanoids, the progenies of the relatively tranquil natural aquatic ecosystem in the underbelly of the main island. Their advanced cooperative communes were accessible only through a concealed entrance that opened and closed like the mouth of a starfish into a maze of canals, tunnels, natural pathways that led to cooperative communal caverns; marvels of advanced civil engineering; oxygenized underground caverns, virtual air pockets with simulated sunlight, climate controls, and sea water purification facilities.

They were not primates or hominids, beasts or monsters, animals, or creatures but highly advanced, civilized humanlike beings with a strong sense of nurturing family and community, a uniform code of tolerant behavior, a natural repulsion to violence and the futility and insanity of war but inherently instilled with a strong and uncompromising sense of survival as a species in harmony with Nature.

Well-meaning cultural anthropologists and other non-obtrusive observers and academic researchers, without wishing to alter any environment or an inhabitant's behavior, might rarely glimpse the Aquarians, almost silently foraging and gathering natural vegan nutriments from the main island's thick vegetation, communicating with each other telepathically. However, these docile, peace-loving humanoids seem to instinctively know that the mere act of being observed by itself altered the subject's behavior. Inherently shy, they were aware of being constantly monitored, but their telepathic ability to render the observer(s) into a trance-like state while scurrying out of view and erasing the human's memory of the viewing vanished all verifiable evidence of their existence.

By various reports, real, imagined, or pure fiction, there was not a trace of scientific evidence that such humanoids, hominids, or cryptids ever existed. This did not deter ardent mythologists, conspiracy theorists, publicity seekers, paranormal special effects camera crew and sound technicians, carnival side-show clairvoyants, hustlers and industry-wide sundry scam artists from fleecing a gullible public for ill-gotten quick financial gain and undeserved celebrity; those individuals obtaining riches and fame based on already being rich and famous and those pointlessly arguing a negative by employing switch logical fallacies as "Arguing from Ignorance" (Latin; argumentum ad ignorantiam); "that which cannot be proven cannot therefore be disproven."

Various eyewitnesses without credible references or any reliable evidence described the Aquarians as being as tall as trees or as short as pygmies, having the muscular girth of a gorilla or slender as a pole, a hairy face and ferocious growl, the face of Helen of Troy and unable to speak above a whisper. Typically, these human observers regularly confuse fictitious with factitious.

The worst of predatory humans derived a living by hunting Bigfoot to capture and kill one or more as trophy evidence. It asserted that Sasquatch was a "*cousin*" to the Aquarian. The Aquarians threatened civil legal action through their human attorney, the prominent litigator Alexandre Begré, declaring that no family relationship existed between themselves and any or all ape-like hominids, demanding that the slanderous defamation "cease" until conclusive scientific DNA samples could be provided as proof.

When the first of the explorers arrived to conduct geological surveys of the main island and plot the land for destructive commercial development despite protests from various ecological and environmental protection organizations, the Aquarians "blended" with the trees, grasslands, and skyline as shadow people. But when hordes of foreigners crowded endlessly onto their homeland demanding more living space and breathing room and developed sophisticated Aquarian-detection technology, the indigenous Humanoids were threatened with forced accommodation, assimilation, or annihilation. But Aquarians chose a clandestine and cultural *taboo* alternative to countering humanity's genocidal campaign with all-out violent reprisals or fleeing back into their guerrilla fighter tunnels and caverns; assuming human-like physical appearance to "blend" and inter-breed with the "deplorables" and diffuse, erode, and eradicate the degenerative human bloodline. "That criminally destructive and diseased gene pool begs for complete and total eradication for the sake of the planet," concluded the Aquarian Grande Council in Executive Session well ahead of the siege of its first invaders.

Chapter Four

YOU CAN'T GET THERE
FROM HERE.

"What difference does it make to the dead,
the orphans, and the homeless, whether
the mad destruction is wrought under the
name of totalitarianism or the holy name
of liberty or democracy?"

—Mahatma Gandhi.

"The gladdest movement in human life is a
departure into unknown lands."

—Sir Richard Burton.

THE NEW AGE PIONEERS were physically
prevented from any exploration of this
newly discovered land mass, not merely by
the Perimeter Islands' natural "blockade"
and the main island's rugged coastline, but
by a strictly enforced unilateral "order of
trespass" issued by The International Court
of Justice until claims of legal ownership
could be entertained and decided.

Fully anticipating errant trespass
violations by terrorist groups and

organizations and secret societies, illegal rights of conquest, marauding bandit countries and outlaw nations; mercenary filibustering military would-be dictators and tyrants and baseless (or groundless?) land grants ("I claim this land in the name of or for. Despite indigenous peoples already residing there.") and international waters limits, lawless conquerors and conquistadors and other false claims, the international community (officially, The Alliance of Nations) moved swiftly and without the usual delays and rancor to secure the sanctity and (presumed) uninhabited sovereignty of the area.

The Alliance of Nations had proven effective by eliminating the flaws of international peacekeeping coalitions, which, other than commendable international humanitarian efforts, were frequently criticized for their ineffectiveness in preventing worldwide wars, regional armed conflicts, and even internal war crimes like ethnic genocidal cleansing. Often chided as little more than international debating societies, the A.N. created a more open dialogue and either eliminated or reduced (1) factional infighting between nations, (2) selfish self-interest or sovereignty concerns, (3) failure or inability to enforce unilateral decisions or legality under international law, (4) non-compliance by affected nations (5) veto power granted to larger, more powerful nations over votes and decisions against their political agendas as well as dissension and quarreling among the veto power clique created gridlock to international problem solving, (6) decisions and rulings by international courts of justice were unenforceable except by the good will of the litigant parties. (7) member nations declined to contribute funds to the treasury, and (8) member nations declined to participate in either peacekeeping or humanitarian missions.

The ANTF, as a global peacekeeping force, and to maintain a nation's sovereignty, set a timetable not to exceed five (5) years in any country, nation, or territory to avoid the appearance of being an occupying force and to respect territorial sovereignty and self-determination.

The Alliance of Nations Task Force (ANTF) for Peacekeeping Among Sovereignties (PAS) rapidly and smoothly deployed to the Doldrums by dispensing with the usual diplomatic rambling, loquacious debates, self-aggrandizing posturing, and veto power abuse by professional politicians, diplomats, and bureaucrats. The international military coalition worked unusually well together, displaying none of the jealousies and rivalries between commanders, service branches, and national allegiances, overcoming language barriers, cultural differences, and even age and gender biases.

The task force command was divided among Major General Erich von Schvinghammer (Land), Vice Admiral Amanda Danziger (Sea) and Air

Marshal Aung San Maung (Air) the latter two who negotiated an ironclad agreement with PAS Command Headquarters that barring firsthand humanitarian rescue operations or other exigent circumstances, there would be no boots on the ground land troops, an agreement aimed directly at restraining the fame and glory seeking Prussian.

Schvinghammer, a notoriously strac and stern Martinet, was exceedingly proud of his long, distinguished military career spanning years in conspicuous and prominent command assignments around the globe and never shy of vainglorious, exaggerated war stories.

Yet the rank of field marshal had always eluded him and, he thought, unfairly. From his childhood days in military boarding schools—he was a volunteer, never a conscript—through his earliest days as a cadet. As a junior officer, he always believed himself Field Marshal material. He'd certainly heard the loud whispers dismissing him as just another politically connected desk general without a minute of combat field experience. He simply discounted them as typical petty jealousies from the bootlicking, apple-polishing, over-eager military clique. Few, if anyone, be they active military staff, veterans, civilians, or political operatives, could dispute the general's military bearing and commanding presence, his close-cropped graying hair, white sidewalls, imposing stature contained in a broad-shouldered, barrel-chested six-foot-three-and-a-half-inch frame, arrogance, and self-confidence. Furthermore, his Prussian Junker lineage and military ancestry added a most impressive pedigree to his credentials. Burst with pride whenever family, his few close friends, and sycophantic admirers likened him to the ruthless Iron Chancellor, Prince Otto von Bismarck, who had unified the various German states into the German Empire. Conversely, it angered him intensely when compared for his striking physical resemblance to the World War I field marshal and second president of the German Weimar Republic, Paul von Hindenburg who while slipping in and out of aged senility facilitated 12 years of cruel NAZI dictatorship, genocidal barbarism and world conquest when he reluctantly appointed Adolf Hitler chancellor of Germany's Third Reich in January 1933 and conveniently died of old age August 2, 1934 to make Hitler absolute dictator by his merging the two offices into one as Fuhrer.

Having twice been passed over by ANTF for promotion to lieutenant general, his career had been blocked and his ambitions frustrated. So twice he had "retired" from active duty to his chicken farm to spite the ANTF, having called his bluff of "Field Marshal or else!" Now he was on his military campaign, his final tour of duty, and more determined than ever to ascend to the pinnacle of command, even if it was ostensibly a peace mission.

He had, in previous periods of active duty, promoted his five sons to his General

Staff as adjutants and aides-de-camp with shameless nepotism. Still, Mazie, his timid and ever-compliant traditional army wife, his grateful heel-clicking sons, social-climbing daughters-in-law, and even his numerous adoring grandchildren would always give the intimidating general a wide berth whenever he swaggered into a room in his full-dress uniform, affecting the appearance of a Caesar-like conquering general with transparent imperial aspirations.

His icy glare from beneath thick, bushy eyebrows and a permanent deep frown extending down to his jutting square chin was known to cause even superior army officers, political tyrants, and all levels of authority to tremble in his wake. His embroidered general's hat and gawdy uniform, having been personally designed and sewn by his ever-supportive Mazie, would have brought severe rebuke if worn by a junior officer. And his thick eyebrows and thick walrus mustache would never be tolerated if worn by subordinate soldiers.

This time, however, the ANTF caved in and relented under his threat of a third and final retirement and promoted him to lieutenant general, giving him equal rank and status with Danziger and Maung.

Privately uttering old school chauvinistic attitudes, he deeply resented having to share command "with those damn women who deserved no military positions beyond military wives, nurses, office workers, and camp followers," Schvinghammer compromised, swallowed his pride, and bit his tongue to accept one last military command and mission to earn the rank of Field Marshal.

A peacekeeping mission was as foreign to the General as some distant land in another solar system in an alien galaxy. Schvinghammer desired nothing less than a war of conquest that would earn him the accolades and praise, the medals of valor, combat ribbons, badges, and medals required, even if he had to award them to himself on the road to the fame and glory that he had always believed was his destiny.

With his regiment dispersed in smaller units along the perimeter isles and performing busy work on troop-carrying ships at sea, the general would need convincing provocation before he could lead his battle-ready troops to liberate New Atlantica from danger. Thus, he called upon his general staff, his eldest son as his executive officer, the second eldest as adjutant, and the remaining two as aid-de-camp and brigade commander to "encourage" an unprovoked attack on unarmed and defenseless humanitarian relief workers. With no time for intelligence analysis and diplomatic debate, the occupational forces landed on the main island to begin their limited conquest of New Atlantica. The northwestern regional dense, almost impenetrable forestland reserve known as The Ybani (Enchanted) Forest and great boulder Granito de Ebano across the northside Darwin Straits were declared strictly off limits by the ANTF military high command but the genocidal search and destroy mission to eliminate any dangerous threats posed by the Aquarians, inhuman indigenous monsters and godless beasts of prey would eagerly be casually condoned by Schvinghammer and his general staff (consisting primarily of his sons) and frequently though covertly encouraged by army's occupation (misnamed liberation) commanders from regimental to platoon level. "If it attacks or threatens, kill it. If it breathes, quarantine it. If it doesn't move, paint it."

Chapter Five

EXTINCTION BY GENOCIDAL MEANS.

───◆───

"Citizens victimized by genocide or abandoned by the international community do not make good neighbors, as their thirst for vengeance, their irredentism and their acceptance of violence as a means of generating change can turn them into future threats."

—Samantha Power.

"Action is the only remedy to indifference: the most insidious danger of all,"

—Elie Wiesel

"We didn't kill them because we couldn't find them. We're not saying they weren't there but we sure as hell didn't see any. I can state unequivocally that we found no evidence whatsoever of their existence, anywhere, no DNA, no hair follicles, no dried clumps of feces, or urine samples, not so much as fossilized skeletal remains. There's no proof that they've ever been here or that Aquarians exist."

—Anonymous Soldier in New Atlantica.

IT WAS NOT IMPOSSIBLE that one or several or perhaps many Aquarians had been shot and killed without a shooter's knowledge, given the mystical or mythological humanoid's innate mystical or mythological abilities to alter appearance or vanish mysteriously from view. Furthermore, without existing physical samples or medical data, any lifeless Aquarian remains would defy identification.

Schvinghammer and his staff, of course, rejected the scouting mission's report and promptly issued a communique. "We KNOW they exist! We've SEEN them, or rather, we've seen the old black and white 8mm film clips of them running through a clearing in the forest. Satellites and low-flying drones have traced their movements. How many haven't seen the plaster casts of their footprints? They're on that island. The scouting party just isn't looking in the right places!"

Naturally, as Schvinghammer and his peers expected, the elitist pseudo-intellectuals, knee-jerk liberals, and the condescending skeptics and cynics would never permit the Schvinghammer communique to go unchallenged without supercilious sarcasm. "Are you all living in some alternate reality? What have you people been smoking? Of course, Bigfoot and the abominable snowman are real. So are leprechauns, elves, vampires, werewolves, and Frankenstein's *Creature*. Humanoids, hominids, cryptic monsters, vicious mammals, and probably dinosaurs all co-exist on a large island floating in the doldrums, an island that until recently was submerged in the ocean. Of course, all contagious diseases are just different strains of influenza and the common cold! And pandemics, epidemics, and endemics are medical frauds invented to sell expensive and addictive pharmaceuticals! Vaccinations are part of a government conspiracy to implant mind-altering microchips into us. Don't forget to leave a nightlight on in your children's bedrooms and check underneath their beds for boogeymen. Do you know where your governments are hiding all the missing socks in the world?"

But Schvinghammer would not be deterred. The professional soldier wanted boots on the ground in full battle gear, ready for combat ASAP! Because the landing craft boats could not maneuver through the perimeter isles and islets, the landing party had to be airlifted into natural clearings on the island, an agonizingly slow process. But not before erudite highbrow university president and professor Anton Gunter-Ellis (AGE), a world-renowned self-proclaimed socialist with two doctorate degrees, one in public administration and another in political science, cashed in political I.O.U.s to join the mission as official ANTF observer and academic advisor. "Goddamn elitist leftwing egghead," raged Schvinghammer, "he's never gotten his hands dirty doing an honest day's labor in his whole nose-in-a-book stuck-up life! He's just a goddamn spy for those ugly-ass butch him-a-nists (Danziger and Maung) to fuck up this entire mission!" Eldest Schvinghammer son and adjutant Wilhelm, along with second son and aide-de-camp Ernst, sanitized their father's profanity and deleted the sexist slurs in the official reports, memos, and communiques in a tireless effort to cleanse the general's public persona and image.

The emotionally detached scientists, meanwhile, were overwhelmed, astonished, and utterly excited by the vast new discoveries on the unexplored terrain. Displaced hominids, clearly non-indigenous, ambled through the dense rain forest uninterested in the unknown non-aquatic mammals and long thought-to-be extinct birds, strange plant life, unidentifiable schools of fish and ocean mammals some vaguely resembling dolphins, manatees, and whales seemed to live harmoniously on land and in the surrounding waters. There were naturally occurring species of fearful-looking carnivores and predators upon the land and in the sea, but not to the point of decimating the food chain.

Traveling with the front-line scouting party, Gunter-Ellis, known as "AGE" or "professor" by the young soldiers providing his safe escort, busied himself by transmitting voluminous scholarly reports from the island when not pestering his guides with incessant questions and long sleep-inducing academic lectures. An ivory tower intellectual, the professor was determined to experience this exciting chance-of-a-lifetime adventure like a bookish Teddy Roosevelt, even if it killed him. He eagerly arrived early to join the expedition, dressed in plain military advisor's attire, including protective armor, just in case the monsters might be real, cordially complying with all the instructions given to him with a warm, friendly smile without question. But weighed down with bulky scientific equipment, he frequently lagged, but the soldiers never once glanced back to see him sweating and panting while thrashing through the thick underbrush. Bringing up the rear so far behind that they frequently wandered off trail to become lost in the unexplored wilderness were the professor's academic research assistant, news media reporters, and crew members. But they were the ones, not the professor or advanced exploration party, to report insubordinate disobedience to ANTF standards and regulations, international environmental code violations, and the criminal acts of harassment, brutality, inhumane mistreatment, and even isolated executions of indigenous beings. In later testimony before an international inquest, Professor Gunter-Ellis stated unequivocally that he had witnessed "nothing but respect for the environment and its inhabitants, ethical behavior and individual high moral compasses within the platoon of kind and compassionate peacekeepers."

However, despite the regimentation and indoctrination of strenuous training, entire platoons of enlisted personnel disagreed with the professor's testimony. Discretely using back channels, they transmitted their anonymous accusations of the slaughter, abuse, and brutality to native beings, aquatic mammals, and birds to investigative journalists, reporters, the inspector general's office, and the high command.

AGE's (Anton Gunter-Ellis) glowing reports of almost pristine behavior and ethical professionalism did not bring surprise to his hosts and guides. All communications and reports, especially those from the professor (AGE), were carefully censured from within the camp by the youngest Schvinghammer son, Karl, posing as Major Johann Schmidt, hourly from the field. And Lieutenant Colonel Karl von Schvinghammer, Major Johann Schmidt, or Captain John Smith, depending upon his covert mission, made sure that the scouting was above reproach.

But the other expeditionary forces serving in the Alliance of Nations' Universal Army 1st Corps, each of its five divisions commanded openly and flagrantly by Schvinghammer's remaining sons, were under no similar restraints or restrictions. Although no written orders were to be issued officially, they were all free and encouraged to search and destroy as part of a surreptitious surge across the island.

"I want this land cleared ASAP," came the order of the day, "for development!" Only immediate family members and closest friends knew of Schvinghammer's "slush fund," supplemental income from commercial developers, and his clique of millionaire investment banker friends.

Employing a standard Motti military tactic from earlier times when war was more prevalent, the light infantry followed the long-range reconnaissance patrols (LRRP) in flanking maneuvers trudged through the thick forests, grasslands, and underbrush unaware of being constantly under the careful eye by the ANTF's select observers led by the youthful international lawyer Alexandre Begré disguised as a low-ranking medical corpsman.

The modern military now comprised more of highly trained specialists and skilled technicians, displeasing the general who openly preferred the O.G. armies of conquest, liberation, war, and survival. He soon grew weary and impatient that a scientific expedition was overshadowing his final and most illustrious military campaign.

Schvinghammer had never liked the peacekeeping missions of the modern military. He was strictly old-world, longing for the days of failed diplomacy when the army was engaged in battle, regime toppling wars of liberation, territorial conquest, covert destabilization of unwanted foreign governments, and the removal of unfriendly leaders even when popularly elected.

Hardly a chess master, he stayed with the tried-and-true battlefront, or in his case, more frequent student uprisings, civil disobedience protests, or organized labor strike-breaking military strategies, his preferred being the wedge, the command post safely in the center behind the field of engagement. Detractors and critics of his embellished war record claimed that it was not uncommon for him to suddenly melt into the ranks of the rear echelon and change into a more inconspicuous uniform of a supply or ordnance senior NCO to avoid capture.

"Goddamn it! I am sick and tired of this panty-waist fuckin' college field trip! Now, lay waste to this overgrown fuckin playground! It's goddamned open season on anything and everything that breathes! "And that includes the goddamn fuckin' scientists and their pinhead schleppers!" the red-faced general raged, his temple veins bulging to near explosion.

Thus, it fell to the conscientious, ever legalistic, and righteously indignant Begré to take decisive action, who, along with but a handful of horrified low-ranking personnel, began to smuggle reports to media sources of wanton acts of merciless brutalities, vicious killings, senseless genocide, and remorseless atrocities. The cruelest atrocities ensued undeterred by the disapproval, dissent, and objections of junior officers, courageous NCOs, enlisted personnel, subject to harsh discipline at the unit level, peer harassment, and for the worst of the squawkers, a code red blanket party, to be unilaterally, unequivocally denied. Civilian whiners and complainers vanished by lagging well behind the rear guard and wandering off the trail to become hopelessly lost in the wilderness, devoured by creatures of the forest, and a faint memory of grieving friends and loved ones. Still, a resolute faction of subversives would undermine the overall mission by smuggling irrefutable eyewitness reports on micro-chipped audio-video recordings of the worst atrocities under the perimeter wire and through the lines to an allegedly biased news media who were extremely eager to report the accusations globally.

The ANTF High Command, urged on by a wave of worldwide outrage, issued the order from the Alliance of Nations (7 members) Directorate to Stand Down.

The German public, tired of General Schvinghammer's militaristic antics, urged their leaders to censure him and distance the nation from his actions. In response, the Bundestag unanimously passed a resolution revoking his Favorite Son status and condemning his conduct in New Atlantic. The Chancellor added that Schvinghammer does not represent contemporary Germany.

Chapter Six

"PATSIES, FALL GUYS AND SACRIFICIAL LAMBS."

———◇◈◇———

"Thou shalt not bear false witness against
thy neighbour."

> —The Ten Commandments,
> Exodus 20:19, and
> Deuteronomy 5:20,
> The Bible.

"I'm just a patsy!"

> —Lee Harvey Oswald.

FROM TOP TO BOTTOM, the international peace-keeping military task force did stand down over Schvinghammer's vociferous protests but remained in a stand-by position as evidence, believed to be planted by army espionage agents, emerged throughout the chain of command to implicate Captain Cassandra McGinnis.

"My name is Cassie, not PATSY!" She was not willing to be anyone's sacrificial lamb; another proverbial fall-on-your-sword, patsy, fall guy. "You people made this mess, not me! And you can clean it up, yourselves!" she shouted in an unusually bold and courageous act of defiance, given her senior officers and her blatant insubordination. If she were facing her accusers at some military installation, on base, in a compound or on the field of combat, SHE would be standing at attention, speaking only in response to questions or commands in her commander's office or an uncomfortable interrogation cell, dressed down, her rank insignia ripped from her uniform, placed in irons, unceremoniously led off by large threatening-looking muscular armed guards, locked behind bars in a small, cramped cold or humid prison cell maybe with vicious criminals and offered few options; to distract the investigation, deflect guilt away from the actual perpetrators, the very ones framing her or face a general courts-martial for mass murder and genocide and certainly do long hard time in a brutal secure military prison far from her following almost certain conviction.

But she was not on a military installation. She was in her own home in the civilian world, talking to civilian press reporters before a live camera crew. She also knew with certainty that the AI ANTF military lacked jurisdiction to arrest her on private property. Civilian police, also, under the AI ANTF authority, would require an arrest warrant or probable cause just to hold her for transfer to military officers. For now, she was freely sharing her own story with sordid details for public sympathy and a fair hearing with the general population, civilians, and military.

Suddenly stepping into her life was the passionate pleader for justice, the brightest star of celebrity (international) attorneys, Alexandre Begré with his dream team of defense attorneys. He had been the prominent covert whistle-blower, the recent and socially privileged law school graduate who ambitiously and quickly assembled a dream team volunteer corps of celebrity criminal defense lawyers and social activists quickly galloping to Cassie's rescue, now to be known for the record as, The Universal Armed Forces v Cassandra McGinnis, CPT, UAF, ANTF.

"All right, Counsellor, you're up." She whispered, sliding behind the brash young lawyer to give him center stage. Wisely, she would not speak again without her attorney at her side until after the verdict was delivered.

Begré and his team blocked the doorway against any attempted arrest or harassment of his astonished client. Then the brash, passionate, youthful young lawyer delivered the prolix. "We are here, pro bono, all of us, because of the gross injustice and baseless unfounded, corrupt, and cowardly lies manufactured against this brave honorable dedicated soldier and flawlessly honest young officer whose only offense seems to be her valiant service and complete devotion to the defense of our liberties, freedom and very lives from the evil forces seeking unjust, unwarranted, and illegal unilateral power over individual, national, and international sovereignty. The only criminals in this slanderous defamation of Captain McGinnis's here-to-now unblemished military record are the genocidal savages who have falsely and viciously implicated Captain McGinnis for their wrongdoings." He railed contemptuously without fear of reprisals.

Then he and his dream team stepped inside to confer with their nearly universally pilloried and maligned client, Cassie McGinnis, to begin the kitchen table consultation.

"Are you guilty of any of these charges?" the elder, veteran lawyer Bertram Dawson asked pointedly, taking the lead.

"Of course not!" she snapped back without hesitation.

"Don't lose your composure," advised Astrid Nilsson, well-versed in preparing witnesses for trial. "Trial lawyers count on that."

"Don't worry about any of that. Astrid will work with you on your demeanor with acting and modeling classes." Begré then rose from his chair, palms flat down on the table, his eyes fixed on Cassie, swiftly reclaiming his position as lead counsel. "But you won't be testifying."

"Won't the judges then assume I'm guilty, that I'm hiding something?"

"The judges cannot give any weight to your silence as an admission of guilt." Interjected Malika Bello, "strong-willed and determined," and the brightest of the eager young associates, anxious that the other team members do not overshadow her legal abilities and contributions.

"No one can force your testimony." Another associate quickly added, "Just keep silent and let the attorneys do their job."

"If you honestly neither participated in nor had knowledge of any of these atrocities," Begré paced already setting the tone for his upcoming performance, "I'll have you fully acquitted of all these ridiculous criminal charges within a matter of a days and well on your way to collect the riches and spoils from your disreputable prevaricating accusers in civil hearings with your reputation fully restored"

"Are you really that good?"

"Are you really that innocent?"

"I'm completely innocent." She said confidently and with composure.

"I'm that good. Now let's get you acquitted and a lot of money in damages."

"You can remain here," Malika said to Cassie in a kind, reassuring voice as the conference ended. "You won't be awaiting trial in some bleak, dark military stockade. "We've had you placed on house arrest. I'm sure you find it much more comfortable and restful here. And there are no intrusive, scary-looking guards at the door. "We're all available if you need anything."

Then the lawyers filed through the front door, returning to their plush uptown offices to map their strategy.

In a few short weeks as she'd been promised her, Captain Cassandra McGinnis was being tried by a serious-minded tribunal of military justice, looking innocent and demure, the stylish work of one of the professional make-up artists hired by Astrid Nilsson but still very much on trial for mass murder, facing the death penalty or life imprisonment at hard labor hanging over her as army Captain Cassandra McGinnis.

Her face revealing little emotion after many hours of dramatic training, she sat quietly while Begré dazzled all with his "trickle down false accusations of misplaced guilt, blame, shame, and frame" to the lower echelons of command. The defense countered by deflecting the focus of the trial, even vaguely but delicately alluding to the prosecutorial misconduct with a top-down war crimes conspiracy and subsequent cover-up.

Bertram Dawson's attempt to have the corps commander, Lt. Gen. Erich von Schvinghammer, himself indicted for the New Atlantica genocidal murders and atrocities in absentia had gone down in flames before the International Court of Justice with accompanying censures. The other lawyers on the team, Astrid Nilsson leading them, insisted to Begré that "Old Bert," the Lion of the Courtroom, his celebrated many courtroom triumphs well behind him, was slipping. Begré reluctantly agreed to sideline him, relegating him to the oft-ignored role of senior legal advisor.

"We've seen these sordid frame-ups before, and we've seen patsies bearing the brunt of the guilt throughout history."

"This is NOT the Dreyfuss case, Counsellor." One weary-looking tribunal judge chided him.

"No, it's not, or I'd have him acquitted, too." The young barrister stated arrogantly, barely acknowledging the interruption.

"You're getting ahead of yourself, Councilor." The same judge snapped back.

"You're quite right, Sir, for if I am permitted to digress, I'll probably solve the Lindbergh baby kidnapping and the disappearance of the Roanoke Colony."

"Move on!" the chief judge barked.

The General's staff somehow miraculously escaped indictment, and the regimental officers, orders, and records were subpoenaed. The various units attempted to bury defense with superfluous data. Still, a corps of social activists, volunteers, and interns, calling themselves with self-effacing humor, pack rats, office vermin, and paper shredders, chewed through the paperwork, extricating the relevant information with dizzying speed.

Smoothly and handily impeaching the credibility of all the prosecution witnesses, destroying the manufactured case against his client, he decisively, and conclusively impugned the corrupt motives, personal agendas and questionable integrity of the prosecution's charges, exposing perjurious testimony and having false evidence rejected out of hand by the judicial panel of judges, he charmed the spectators with his polished charisma as the whole world seemingly watched on the edge of their chairs.

"You are the regimental commander, are you not, Colonel?" He began his cross-examination while still seated at the long Defense table.

"That's right. I commanded two battalions. The LRRPs were first on the main island. Then my regiment landed."

"So, you established the beachhead for the occupation forces," Begré said, declaratively.

"There was no damn beachhead. It's virtually impossible to do a sea-based landing on that island!" the colonel snapped back at him.

"The troops had to be airlifted onto the island, an agonizingly slow and deliberate process by chopper. We couldn't drop by parachutes, too many trees, and other hazards. The clearings were small and scattered about the island, and logistics had trouble coordinating without risking the safety of troops from sniper attacks. And for your information, Counselor, it wasn't an occupation! It was a liberation!" The colonel protested indignantly.

Begré, a smug smile on his face, rose from his chair and approached the witness. "Yes, of course. I stand corrected." The chief judge gaveled the courtroom amid scattered laughter and snickering. "You were liberating the island from what, insects, migrating whales, and penguins?" Begré taunted.

"We were responding to a clear and present danger on the island." The colonel pointedly replied without pause or emotion. "The air force came under fire from the island."

"Yes, we've all heard how some low-flying reconnaissance flight mysteriously came under fire from some ground-based unknown unseen unidentifiable invisible phantom enemy. Doesn't that seem rather implausible, Colonel? That's a rhetorical question; you needn't respond." Continuing, he asked the agitated witness, "Did you or anyone under your immediate command locate and identify any surface-to-air weaponry while liberating this erroneously thought-to-be uninhabited island?"

"Not to my knowledge." The colonel answered quietly.

"So, what the hell were you doing there?"

"We were ordered there to preserve peace and tranquility!" the Angry, red-faced colonel shouted.

"To ensure peace and tranquility for an uninhabited island?"

"It was initially thought to be uninhabited. Those reports were premature and incorrect." Argued the colonel, emphatically.

"And this pointless surge took place despite the High Command unilaterally commanding there to be no boots on the ground?"

"That order, as we all know, was rescinded!" barked the witness.

"Yes, it was, Colonel, which made it open season on all non-human forms of life." Then, turning back toward the defense table before the prosecution could object or the judges could chastise him, he loudly and clearly said, apologetically, "Withdrawn." Then, seemingly as an afterthought, asked, "Who assigned a REMF (the derogatory term meaning rear echelon generally non-combative support soldiers or more graphically by combat troops, rear echelon mother fucker) ordinance captain to command a seasoned, jaded, combat-weary company of pissed-off grunts (slang, infantry soldier)?"

"Counsel!" one of the judges scolded him.

"My abject apologies to the court. Yes, I know language." He smirked; the emphasis upon Cassie's assigned MOS (military occupational status) from this point became the dream team's standard code word throughout the trial.

"I have no idea who assigned her," the colonel barked. "I have far more important things on my mind. Furthermore, Counsellor, may I add that I'm not fond of your descriptive nouns of my brave infantrymen!"

"Those were adjectives, Colonel," Begré advised him with sarcasm. "And I'm done with you."

"The witness may stand down." Stated one of the justices.

"Yes, Colonel, stand down, and THAT was the only wise decision made by command during this entire fiasco." He uttered, risking another verbal reprimand.

Next, Begré attacked the credentials of the regimental staff psychiatrist.

"Doctor, are you a board-certified psychiatrist?"

"Yes," the doctor replied calmly, "I'm a practicing psychiatrist."

"Well, with a little more practice, perhaps you'll be ready to go out on your own." Begré chided.

The doctor held up his hand to the judges' latest reprimand, unfazed by the lawyer's friendly tease, fully ready to engage him.

"And I would hope as much for you, Counsel."

"Imagine the two of us released upon an unsuspecting world." The brash young lawyer was entertaining a normally staid courtroom while putting the cordial witness further at ease. "But these are not for small minds to ponder. I would boldly presume, Doctor, that you are quite familiar with the mental and emotional stresses, the trauma of combat."

"I am well acquainted with combat-related PTSD, post-traumatic stress disorder, and have treated more soldiers for it than you can imagine."

"You have no idea what I can imagine, Doctor. But be that as it may, have you treated soldiers in the field?"

"Not personally in the field, no. But I've seen the medical reports of those who have."

Begré then entered the Alpha Company, commanded most recently by the defendant, filed reports without objection into evidence, challenging it as exculpatory, and demanding why the prosecution had not previously made available in discovery. Barely pausing, he directed more demanding questions to the regimental psychiatrist.

"You haven't read these reports?" Begré feigned astonishment.

"I don't believe they've been brought to my attention for review." The psychiatrist answered quietly.

Begré, reading from selected files, his outrage barely concealed, offered to enlighten both the psychiatrist and the tribunal, chronicling a shocking list of soldiers mentally unfit for duty, along with a half dozen names belatedly identified as psychotic killers.

Once the courtroom gasps dissipated, the psychiatrist partially rose from his chair, shouting, "You can't saddle me with these aberrations of company behavior, Mr. Begré, the psychiatrist boomed over the courtroom gasps, "I was never made aware of any of these isolated cases."

"Neither, for the record, was Captain McGillis. And yet, she's on trial for her very life!" Begré thundered back at the witness. "Can you give us one reason, just one solitary reason, a medical reason, why Alpha Company was not disbanded, its members debriefed and reassigned and those most damaged, the ones afflicted by combat-related mental and emotional stress, traumatized and victimized; why they were not mercifully and humanely in treatment as a danger to themselves and others?" he shouted, his words more of a demand than a question.

"None of that was under my direct authority!" the witness angrily responded.

"No, because you were much too safe and comfortable in your regimental ivory tower to be bothered by the invisible injuries and horrors of war!" As the witness abandoned his professional demeanor and the prosecution's shouts echoed throughout the chamber, Begré curtly concluded, "I'm quite finished with your dereliction of duty, Doctor, and the prosecution's concealment of exculpatory evidence."

The tribunal judges, while again censuring Begré quickly and sternly, overruled the prosecution's defensive outrage. Simultaneously, they summarily dismissed the psychiatrist's outcries of injury to his professional credentials.

Then, noting the late hour, the able defense attorney surprised the entire courtroom and reporters by excusing himself from the proceedings and turning the examinations over to his associates. There were excited murmurs in the courtroom and Cassie was alarmed. It was then only mid-week.

"Why is he leaving?" A fearful Cassie demanded.

Astrid slid into the empty seat next to her, comforting her quietly as the chief judge adjourned the courtroom. "He'll be back in a couple of days."

"In a couple of days? I need him here, now!"

"This is child's play for him." Shrugged an associate.

"Child's play? I'm on trial for my life!" she blurted.

"He knows that." Said Malika calmly.

"These are the minnows. He's casting his line for the big fish. Don't worry, Captain. We've got this." Astrid reassured her.

Begre' was neither abandoning Cassie nor the trial. He locked himself inside his luxurious hotel suite, preparing for the most critical final witness and the imperative and fateful summation.

In his absence, the dream team performance of Malika and Astrid was exemplary.

On Thursday and Friday, Cassie watched quietly as the well-versed team performed proficiently by thoroughly impeaching and dispatching witnesses, some cited for perjury, their recollections conflicted, contradicting each other regarding dates and events, and frequently confusing Cassie's orders and tour of duty with her predecessor.

Flimsy evidence was tossed out of court, and the judges overruled numerous prosecution objections, which were typical and routine for them.

Old Bert redeemed himself by having several prosecutorial issues (disputed questions of fact) overturned.

Then Cassie was driven back to house arrest, ordered to rest and not to think of the trial during a quiet weekend. Everyone enjoyed a peaceful weekend, but Alexandre Begré and the final witness for the prosecution. They both studied the transcripts and the minutest facts of the case day and night.

Chapter Seven

"BEGRÉ V. SCHVINGHAMMER."

"Laws are spider webs through which the
big flies pass, and the little ones get
caught."

—Honore de Balzac.

"The trouble with law is lawyers."

—Clarence Darrow.

ON MONDAY AFTERNOON FOLLOWING a long lunch break
on the final day of testimony, the *People*
(prosecution) having *rested* their case, the
Dream Team's heaviest ammunition, young
Oxford-schooled lead attorney Alexandre,
finally returned *to grace the courtroom*,
a snide court reporter noted to a larger-
than-usual audience, and personally dispose
of the primary accuser, the battalion
commander, LTC Karl von *Schvinghammer*.

"For my clarification," Begré asked with
a smirk as he swaggered toward the witness,
"am I now addressing Lieutenant Colonel
Karl Schvinghammer, Major Johann Schmidt,
or Captain John Smith?"

"Lieutenant Colonel Karl Helmut Wolfgang von Schvinghammer, if you please, Sir, just as I swore when I took this witness stand!" the witness thundered with annoyance.

"I've met your alter egos and they're quite charming. You, not so much." Then, addressing the bench, he asked, "Permission to treat this one personality as hostile?"

"Counsel, go ahead, but do so with more respect," barked the chief judge.

"So, Lieutenant Colonel, we are yet to understand why a staff ordinance officer with absolutely no previous combat experience would ever be assigned to command infantry soldiers."

"Those orders were cut by Division HQ, neither by me nor by my request. I had absolutely nothing to do with it. Division personnel assigned her in error would be my guess." Karl squirmed.

"Why was the former C.O., that is, commanding officer, replaced? Was he indicted for some military infraction through normal routine rotation incompetence, possibly? Would you care to guess about that, also?"

Karl turned suddenly serious, explaining with sadness, "Captain Michelson, K.I.A., Killed in Action, body recovered. Multiple fragmentation. Tragic. The preliminary investigation concluded Friendly Fire."

"That doesn't sound very damn friendly to me. But it does explain the confusion." Begré rebutted with sarcasm.

"I believe they've closed the investigation. There isn't any question about it. What confusion?" the lieutenant colonel parried.

"Oh, the minor little mix-up during testimony. It's hardly worth mentioning," Begré said casually, "it's just that three, maybe four witnesses from Alpha Company, enlisted soldiers under oath, mind you, initially swore that it was Captain Michelson rather than McGinnis who used terms like search and destroy, herd up those hominids, get rid of mutha fuckas, mass burials, innocent comments like that. Of course, they recanted on redirect. But then, as one would expect, the defense demanded to recross. I've been informed that you were not present for those testimonies, and I'd been called away on some unrelated business," Begré spoke in a more cordial tone as if talking to a friend, "but I understand the recantations and confusion went on for two or three hours. Personally, I don't understand how anyone confuses Michelson with McGinnis, the words don't even rhyme or sound the least bit similar," a pall of silence fell over the proceedings. Cassie listened intently, the expression on her face almost asking, "He's acting disingenuous. He's up to something."

Begré leaned across the witness stand like a neighbor chatting to a friend over a fence, "and how can anyone get a rugged-looking male like Kevin Michelson confused with such an attractive young woman like Cassie McGinnis? Well, it's a mystery to me. They just didn't seem, at least according to the transcripts, able to distinguish between a male C.O. or a woman C.O. or accurately recall which one ordered the damn search and destroy mission, Michelson, or McGinnis. Now, that's speculative. Friendly Fire? Fratricide? The killing of one's brother-in-arms. You mean assassination, fragged, don't you, Karl? Wasn't he killed by a grenade in his tent, possibly by one of his men, in everyday civilian jargon?"

The calculating lawyer paused waiting, as Karl shifted nervously in his seat, his eyes darting around the room, settling on the prosecution table seeking rescue as the silence in the room reached an agonizing pitch. "I wonder why they didn't simply promote Michelson's second in command, his X.O. (Executive Officer), Lieutenant, now what is his name? As battalion commander, you would know that Colonel, or do you need to check with your X.O.?"

"Lieutenant Cassidy," Karl answered.

"Yes, Lieutenant Cassidy." Begré continued with sarcasm. "First Lieutenant Chris Cassidy, very popular with the rank-and-file EMs, NCOs, too, I hear. He's been recently promoted to captain, as I understand."

"We made a mistake in thinking he wasn't previously ready for command. He's more than qualified to be C.O. And it's Thomas, Tom, not Chris!"

"Sorry, I expected another M name, like maybe Mueller." Begré mused while pausing for his amusement. "Alpha Company had three commanders in a very short time, from Michelson to McGinnis to Cassidy. Of course, we're all sorry to hear of Captain Michelson's untimely demise." Then, he interjected complacently, "How very tragic. But there was friction between them, Michelson and Cassidy, was there not? It got heated occasionally, but never erupted into violence?"

"I never heard any rumors like that," Karl murmured very quietly, evasively.

"Oh yes, Cassidy was in line for C.O. before YOU anointed Michelson, an old family friend, I've heard. But let's not plant our feet there. We've lingered long enough. We should at least reexamine the wisdom of your supposed guess, Lieutenant Colonel? Karl winced at Begre's continued sarcasm as the lawyer suddenly, surprisingly swung back to Cassie's transfer. "Alpha Company is a unit under your battalion command, I believe. Now, Lieutenant Colonel Karl Helmut Wolfgang von Schvinghammer, Battalion Commander, now, for our collective enlightenment, why do you suppose HQ would plant an ordinance officer without a CIB (Combat Infantry Badge) to lead a combat infantry company? Was that to spy upon a peacekeeping mission?"

"Our units don't spy on each other!" Karl protested loudly.

"Objection!" shouted one of the prosecutors. "The witness is being asked to speculate."

"This entire inquisition is speculative." Begré quickly responded, shouting over the objection. "The High Command spied on REMF's until they found a patsy!"

Argumentative! Inflammatory!" came the angry expected prosecution protest.

"It's a trial, Sir, not an inquisition!" another prosecutor shouted.

The tribunal judges said nothing. They watched Begré as if watching an actor's soliloquy.

"With all due respect to the honorable tribunal judges, this entire monkey trial has been speculative, speculating that it would be easy to frame an inexperienced, uninformed, unenlightened rear echelon staff officer and plant her into a doomed-to-fail mission."

This time, the heated objection came from the witness: "Crazy conspiracy theories, without a shred of truth to any of them!" Karl shouted, losing all poise.

"Come on, Oswald, get off the sixth floor!" a prosecutor taunted, alluding to the JFK assassination, to an outburst of laughter and catcalls.

"This is a conspiracy, a family conspiracy to provoke military incursion on a peaceful land mass of vegetation and docile aquatic animal-life for the profiteered publicity, exaggerated fame, unearned glory, and unlawful enrichment of the Schvinghammer Family!"

All but the defense gasped loudly; the hero of no wars was under assault.

"Bullshit!" Karl again lost his self-control. The bench agreed, showing disapproval on their faces and with the sound of the gavel. "There's a mountain of testimony and evidence against this woman! She's hardly innocent of anything, mass murder, especially!" Karl yelled, jumping up from his chair, pointing an accusatory finger at Begré.

"Character assassination! Defamation! Slander!" shouted the entire prosecution in unison.

"The court agrees. Objection sustained. Move on, Counsellor."

"We're an entire island of plants, Colonel," Begré shouted, addressing the witness as Colonel for the first time to the shock of everyone, "You were planted twice. I was placed as a medical corpsman with minimal CRP skills. I believe I bandaged your clerk's typing finger one day. God knows who else was planted. So many of us planted right under your damn gardener's nose, Corporal Lee Font Begré, Medical Corps, I'm not some spy network spook. Major Johann Schmidt and Captain John Smith report to Lieutenant Colonel Karl Schvinghammer, who then reports to whom, big brother Wilhelm or Ernst Schvinghammer, or do you all then report directly to the very top of the familial ladder, to your…mother, Mazie Schmidt-Schvinghammer?"

Finally, Begré, turning his back on witnesses and jurists, motioned toward the rear of the room. "Corporal, may we have the battalion—the Alpha Company morning and daily action reports to place into evidence now, please?" Begré called to the rear of the room as heads turned in that direction. The judges craned their necks, peering toward the back of the room for a non-existent corporal. Throughout the courtroom, all eyes were focused on Karl von Schvinghammer on the witness stand.

"There's nothing there to implicate me or my family! We didn't put anything in writing! Those transcripts are goddamn fuckin' fabrications!" Karl, leaping to his feet again, shouted, instantly incriminating himself.

"Karl, sit the hell down and shut the fuck up! Nothing is incriminating in the goddamn reports!" Hans shouted from the rear of the gallery.

"We're done. Defense rests." Bergé smirked, turning away from Karl.

Stepping back to the defense table, he smiled at the defendant, who glanced around the courtroom, a worried, befuddled look on her face. Begre' leaned closer, whispering almost silently in her ear, "Psyche!"

Cassie blushed and stifled a giggle, wondering if her attorney had not breached or, at least, bent some legal ethical standard. She bit her lip, clenched her teeth, and said nothing.

Her attorney's summation was unusually brief and concise. The prosecutors, the media and public agreed, had lost its case with its arrogance and cockiness, contradictory testimony, dishonest lying witnesses, a family-wide conspiracy, bungled subsequent cover-up, frame-up of an innocent and honorable army officer and especially the reasonable doubt surrounding the cold-blooded battlefield fragging (murder by fragmentation grenade exploding in his tent or quarters) of an army commanding officer, possibly by his second-in-command and perhaps even others under and over his direct command.

The not guilty verdict, in fact, "complete innocence," an astute news commentator observed, was so clear, so evident that the jurists never retired to deliberate. Any decision other than full acquittal would have been met universally with a public worldwide outcry of craven injustice, only to be immediately overturned by the next higher legal authority without dissent.

Cassie immediately hugged all the members of her dream team with unrestrained gratitude at the second the verdict was announced before Malika Bello could tell her, "Oh, Captain, we're not finished yet."

A surprised Cassie uttered, "No?"

Highly unusual for a military trial, the team followed with a lucrative civil suit for false charges, persecution, sexual discrimination, harassment, defamation of character, and other multiple personal injurious damages, finally settled out of court by both the Universal Army and the Alliance of Nations presidium. Cassie McGinnis was quietly promoted, skipping over more senior officers, eventually to the rank of full lieutenant colonel. She also received a huge, undisclosed financial award and a choice of plush assignments. Unselfishly donating much of the monetary settlement, for appearances' sake as Astrid advised her, establishing a legal fund for women suing for sexual assault and discrimination, a scholarship for young women military cadets, a charitable not-for-profit foundation to battle famine, disease, and illiteracy in third world countries but otherwise she tried to continue her military career quietly. It was not to be. Her unsought global celebrity constantly intruded on her privacy. Eventually, she resigned from the military to pursue a law career and join the dream team at Sirius International Law Group as lead investigator and military advocate. She was designated ad hoc (Latin "as needed"), granting her time to manage her foundation.

And as a reward for his legalistic resurgence during the trial, "Old Bert" Dawson found his once fading career revived as the firm's managing partner.

A nearly unbroken chain of impeached witnesses, many facing subsequent perjury charges, concealed exculpatory evidence, along with allegations from the bench of prosecutorial misconduct, almost rendered a summation from the defense practically unnecessary.

The Corps commander himself, Lt. Gen Erich von Schvinghammer, fully insulated thousands of miles away in a lofty well-guarded office and protected by his rank and prestige, never faced any criminal charges for the island atrocities. But he coolly allowed the youngest two of his regimented spit-and-polish military schooled five sons, Hans and Karl to be sacrificed, protecting their older brothers for the good of the order as the general went on another long sabbatical well out of the glare of negative publicity to commiserate with a new acquaintance, the professorial Anton Gunter-Ellis, a peculiar pairing of nationalistic militarist and elitist brahmin.

The notoriety of the arrest and trial of Hans and Karl, both already guilty in the world court of public opinion, devastated the matronly Mazie, nearly shattering her weak heart. But she took it in stride, calmly and softly consoling her brave men that they need not be in prison long if they behaved honorably and brought no further shame to the family name. She promised that their father loved them dearly, if distantly, and that they would be aptly rewarded when they eventually emerged from prison with modest lifetime stipends and comfortable cottages in the distant countryside where they could cause no further embarrassment to the general. For now, as men of valor, not whimpering cry-babies, they were expected to fall on their swords silently and dutifully. Then Mazie rose, kissed her sons on the foreheads, turned, and slipped into her bedroom, quietly closing the door behind her.

Mainly for moral support and family loyalty, but without any visible warmth or affection, first son Wilhelm provided his younger brothers with a limousine and personally escorted them to the courthouse, but did not remain for the sentencing hearing, as it might appear that he was condoning their criminal behavior. Ernst then arrived soon afterwards to succeed Wilhelm. He too sat stoically in the last row of courtroom pews. When asked to address the court on behalf of the youngest scions, he silently demurred and stole from the courtroom.

The evening following the sentencing, third son Heinrich held a press conference at the front gate of the Schvinghammer grounds, read a brief perfunctory statement remonstrating the war crimes of Hans and Karl, issued the family's heartfelt condolences and sympathies to the victims, then pivoted and walked swiftly to the manor, the guards shutting the gate behind him.

No further comments would ever be made. Hans and Karl were abruptly and forever disowned and cast out of family hearth and home at that very moment, their names never again to be spoken in public or private.

Their father, Erich von Schvinghammer, suddenly and inexplicably promoted to full general and facing no criminal charges himself nor recriminations from the news media and courts of public opinion, departed the secure sanctuary of his manor to commiserate with Gunter-Ellis, unscrupulous billionaire J.J. "Jake" Gillis and other sordid opportunistic adventurers in an undisclosed secluded redwood blanketed mountain resort.

Chapter Eight

THE DIVIDED HOUSE OF RUTHERFORD.

"Nothing hurts the affections of both parents and children so much as living too closely connected and keeping up the distinction too long."

—Thomas Paine.

"When Religion and Royalty are swept away, the people will attack the great, and after the great, they will fall upon the rich."

—Honore de Balzac.

THE ENTIRE NEW ATLANTICA Archipelago was smoothly ceded to "that annoying, obnoxious and irritating little bastard Sean Fidwitter," begrudgingly from the Marquess of Rutherford by descent, resulting from his persistent and infuriating paternity lawsuit augmented with the writ of summons to Parliament filed by best friend Alexandre Begré thereby further scandalizing the hedonistic duke's long tumultuous marriage to the artificial, pretentious and untitled Margaret Stanton, who was in love more with the title than the man, at times barely tolerating the man, a union producing no heirs, heiress nor happiness. To rid himself of the persistent reminder of his youthful indiscretion and social blunder with Sean's single mother, Crystal Chandelier (nee Christine Murphy), a very flexible exotic dancer and home entertainment hostess well acquainted with legions of intimate royal patrons, friends, and admirers, both male and female, the duke was only too eager and willing to free himself of an unwanted son, uninhabited island, and an unforgiving wife with the mere stroke of a pen and the seal of a notary.

"I don't care how you do it, but that obnoxious little bastard must be dealt with once and for all!" the duchess demanded during a late-night rant. "You're a duke. Why can't you just make him disappear?"

"Because it's against the law to murder people—even by proxy," the long-suffering duke pleaded with his relentless, status-seeking wife, trying to reason with her. Then, muttering mostly to himself and out of her earshot, "My dear, I don't have those contacts. You should have married a royal highness, not some non-hereditary distant relative with an unfunded title."

"Give him something to make him go!" she snapped over her shoulder at him as she strode across the floor into her boudoir, slamming and double-locking the door behind her.

The duke had little to offer. His three other homes, spacious ancestral castles, were seriously decaying and mortgaged— mortgaged to the hilt. He derived his income primarily from rock musicians partying among old family portraits, the cheap canvas cracking, and painting chipping and rusting suits of knight armor with respect for antiquity.

The combined castle and property rentals, along with fewer special appearance ribbon- cutting gratuities, barely allowed the duchess to maintain a facade of living in luxury at the dwindling estates and manor. To the horror of old friends and especially the Duchess, he more recently suffered the indignity of opening his private golf course, polo field, and fox-hunting grounds to the public for whatever fees he might negotiate. His mounting debts continually pushed him back against the plastered, crumbling wall until, in desperation, he entertained several tourist commission entreaties to conduct guided tours of his beloved Rutherford Manor with a donation box placed at the exit turnstile.

In due course, with remarkable speed, the Sirius paralegals traced a legitimate royal land grant deeding the area encompassing the entire New Atlantica archipelago and possibly occurring a few centuries before when a weary-eyed "lookout" on a long-lost caravel, sailing exploration ship, awaiting rescue from larger faster ships with larger crews or the infrequent trade winds mistook a dark shadow upon or just barely beneath the water or maybe a mirage brought about by feverish delusions, thirst, starvation, or even wishful thinking and claiming it as an island in the name of the House of Rutherford. Thinking this land mass worthless and weary of having his legs pulled apart by the Duchess and Sean like a Christmas turkey wishbone, the duke surrendered the entire archipelago to his troublesome son's litigators, Alexandre Begré and Sirius Law Group, in settlement for his one uninhibited wild night of reckless debauchery with Chrystal Chandelier.

"Your Lordship, you are now a man of immense property, a land baron." The lawyer, Alexandre Begre', bowed majestically with comical exaggeration to his best friend, the former Sean Fidwitter, to be known hereafter as the bon vivant Marquess of Rutherford and a perplexed, financially burdened proprietary of the New Atlantica archipelago.

"Oh, not a baron, the lowest rung on the ladder of supercilious pretension, my most esteemed shyster, but a Marquess, a meaningless, powerless, grossly outdated, pompous title of ignominy. Now let's get Sirius, he punned amid a smattering of giggles, scattered laughter, and eye-rolling groans. "What the hell am I supposed to do with a penniless title and worthless island in the goddamn Doldrums?" He raved.

It was indeed a realistic problem, an undeveloped, virtually uninhabited but for a few dozen squatters hiding in the forests, the underbrush and concealed beneath the green canopies on the large island, a few dozen families scattered among the tiny islands and islets, the occasional fishing boat adrift in the calm seas and one over-paid, over-privileged draconian governor, an antebellum-like overseer with a small office staff, a dozen household servants and landscapers, and a coterie of guards keeping a distant and disinterested eye on the boulder colony, Granito de Ebano.

Established a few years before the first scientific exploration and survey of the main island by penologists, overworked and underpaid sociologists, educators, case workers, probation and parole officers, and frustrated urban planners, to the tragic overflow of the world's societal unsolvable problems of humanity, of whom the professionals had thrown up their hands as hopelessly unredeemable. "Not everyone can be rehabilitated." Sighed one exhausted judge, signing permanent ostracization papers creating Granito de Ebano as the official site for recalcitrant offenders. "Perhaps they will learn to live together on a boulder or be eaten by the sea turtles and sharks."

Once dropped by net onto the flat-topped boulder, there was no safe escape from the towering slick-walled boulder but to plunge into the treacherous bone-crushing southside Darwin Straits rapids at the base of the boulder or risk certain death diving into the depths of the equatorial waters below the slippery, forbidding remaining walls. Three months of food and water rations were dropped by parachute. Thereafter, the residents of Granito de Ebano—few dared labeling it the penal work colony that it was—were expected to fend for themselves.

During his long sojourn aboard the Sirius yacht, Sean met frequently with his one-time Oxford roommate, Lef Begré, to discuss his paternal suit settlement.

Sean's admission into a prestigious university had always been a perplexing mystery. Someone of considerable influence had pulled some strings. Few doubted Sean Fidwitter's intelligence; he was extremely bright, quick-witted, and well-read, but never an eager or ambitious student. His tuition was always paid in full, as were his housing costs, books, and other fees, and he was never without a sizable monthly allowance drawn freely and quite regularly from the university cashier's office.

It had once been assumed that his father, the duke, had anonymously been paying the bills to confirm the veracity of the outlandish Rutherford birthright claim. But then, when the duke's financial worries came to light, Sean's source of income, his mother, died during his early childhood of an undisclosed disease, leaving behind only a pile of debts which had been inexplicably absolved.

The errant Duke of Rutherford could be of no assistance to Sean, his lawyers, or creditors either. He had become a debt-ridden fugitive, vanishing under the cover of darkness, absconding with the family jewels, priceless silverware, and the few remaining unsold heirlooms, switching his roadster with a neighborly tradesman for a nondescript work truck and believed to be in perpetual hiding among the last dwindling numbers of once-venerated royal families, diminishing batches of no longer prominent nobility, and now disreputable old-monied aristocracies around the globe. His three inherited castles and his beloved manor slid steadily into disrepair and foreclosure. The new owner of the manor, a crass millionaire of accumulated wealth in discount retail merchandising, allowed her to reside, rent-free, in the distant guest house if she kept unembarrassedly out of sight from his robust crowd of nouveau riche family and friends and refrained from bothering the hired help. Her socialite friends refused to abandon her, discreetly providing her with a fashionable wardrobe and undetectable costume jewelry, buying her lunches and dinners at reasonably priced diners, giving their unused cosmetics into her knockoff handbags and accessories, and bribing stodgy old widowers to escort her to society events, always avoiding being seen conversing with her. Throughout these many travails, the elegant duchess remained a woman of composure, charm, and grace, concealing any feelings of rejection, betrayal, and abandonment in a broken heart that mercifully ended her sorrow three short years later.

Chapter Nine

"THEY'RE LEGAL IF I SAY THEY'RE LEGAL."

———◆———

"Refugees didn't just escape a place. They had to escape a thousand memories until they'd put enough time and distance between them and their misery to wake to a better day."

—Nadia Hashimi.

"It is the obligation of every person born in a safer room to open the door when someone in danger knocks."

—Dina Nayeri.

"No one puts their children in a boat unless the water is safer than the land."

—Warsan Shire.

HAVING EVICTED THE LAST of the salary-grabbing, listless Granito de Ebano governors and staff from the comfortable overseer's residential compound on the northernmost point of the main island, Sean Fidwitter finally moved onto the main island of New Atlantica as the third year of his sole

ownership came to an end. Only two years
remained as an international protectorate
before he would be forced to assume full
responsibility for its population of human
squatters living on the islets or hiding in
its underbrush, grasslands, and forests,
the aquatic creatures, an apocryphal race
of humanlike cryptids labeled Aquarians,
sea life, natural environment, ecology,
and borders. Alexandre Begré and the entire
Sirius Law Group moved temporarily onto
the residential compound of Sean's uneasy
land acquisition. Greater New Atlantica
encompassed archipelago as the whole
excluding Granito de Ebano inexplicably
leased to Jake Gillis as a mining colony
and permanent rehabilitation community
and the wilderness preserve on the main
island's northeastern corner, occupied
and long ago colonized peacefully by the
mysterious, bronze-skinned, towering Ybani
people, thought to be "a lost tribe" of
some unexplored Asian jungle or the last
surviving mutants of a mid-20th Century
unreported nuclear accident on an unchartered
South Pacific atoll or small island and
transported to New Atlantica to conceal the
destruction of their habitat.

Sean disliked-or feared-being alone, so he
generously shared the spacious, luxurious
house with Alexandre, Bert, Astrid, and
Malika, whose associates, office staff,
researchers, and paralegals occupied the
comfortable former staff and security
buildings as offices and small apartments

with a shared kitchen and large dining area. Anchoring the corporate yacht offshore, guarded by the remaining ANTF naval ships, they were forced to hire expensive commercial helicopters to airlift their offices onto the island. The first of a series of free-spending governors anticipating a hurried escape had ordered a landing strip and hangars built to accommodate light aircraft and small corporate jets.

"At least we didn't have to wade ashore like MacArthur in the Philippines." Malika joked as the corporate commuter plane landed safely on the compound.

"A carefully staged photo op." Bert snapped critically.

On one quiet evening when sharing drinks with the partners and senior staff and star gazing by the compound observatory, Alexandre finally asked Sean, "Have you thought about how to manage this archipelago after the A.N. withdraws its military protection and scientific and exploration funding? There's no financial settlement for land management."

"I cannot improve on Nature's management of this archipelago for thousands of years with any human interference," Sean replied. "Seriously, who but me would live on a desolate island in the damn doldrums, anyway?"

"Sean, the world is dangerously overcrowded, hungry for living space. Land is at a premium." Bert advised him. "Soon your island will be overrun by hordes of intruders, invaders, interlopers, spoilers, developers, and squatters like creditors at a debtor's door. How will you protect your borders?"

"With no trespassing signs and concertina wire along the shoreline." Sean replied with flippancy before pausing thoughtfully to ask, "Are you telling me the island is no longer an A.N. protectorate?"

"Time is running out for your archipelago as a protectorate, Sean. All task force troops will be withdrawn in less than two years." Bert patiently explained. "The A.N. charter limits their military presence to five years in any sovereign country, land, or territory to avoid the appearance of an occupation."

"And, if some foreign power invades my island?" Sean asked.

"The task force may return for exigent circumstances only at the sovereign country's request and a majority vote of the A.N. Security Council. However, the A.N. charter prohibits interference in internal affairs."

"Sean, the clock is ticking," Astrid added. "You need to decide soon to declare this a privately owned island, which means you will have to manage it without public funds and grants or open the floodgates to land grants, mass immigration, and the commercial and residential over-development that we all know you deplore so much."

"There's a tree growing on that vacant lot. Quick, let's rip it up by the roots before it spreads!" interjected a paralegal, mocking a familiar Sean Fidwitter mantra, then continued, "Okay, bring in the trucks with the steel, concrete, and asphalt."

Sean was pensive, unusually quiet. Alexandre observed the discussion from a faraway corner in silence and detached curiosity.

"You know, there are entire communities of isolated squatters living illegally on your islands?" Another paralegal read from a scouting report.

"It's my island." Sean asserted in surprising, uncharacteristic dominance. "If I say they're legal, they're legal. And I say they're legal."

"Well, then," Bert nodded, "I guess they're legal residents, your first citizens."

"I never planned to live here alone like some modern-day Robinson Crusoe," Sean said, contemplatively.

"By the terms of the settlement, you cannot legally dispose of it." Astrid further advised. 'You can neither sell nor abandon it nor attempt to bequeath it to another individual or foreign entity. This must now be your primary residence. Otherwise, ownership reverts to the Duke of Rutherford or his estate."

Sean paced the room for a moment before turning to the team with a definitive and surprising announcement.

"I'm opening the entire archipelago, every square meter, especially the uninhabited main island, to immigration," Sean announced, to the group's astonishment. Then, he alarmed them further. "But only to the destitute and homeless, the displaced and dispossessed, the hungry and hopeless."

"That's very commendable but impractical." Bert advised.

"A monumental task!" Malika agreed. "How could you ever implement it?"

"I'm not implementing it, you are!" Sean challenged them. "You, the Alliance, those irritating religious missionaries, the humanitarians, the forest rangers, Green Peace, the International Red Cross and even that cookie selling adorable little girl scouts."

"This isn't going to be pro bono," Astrid rose, "I can promise you!"

Alexandre finally broke his silence. "This island was never to be a permanent residence for the Sirius Law Group, Sean. I am eager to return to practicing international law. In all fairness…"

The other lawyers joined in the discussion, cutting off Alexandre.

"The firm requires a lot more clients, cash flow, and liquidity," Bert said. "Although we could float for a while longer, but not indefinitely."

"My lifestyle requires a lot more than I'm earning here," Astrid added.

Alexandre rose and continued as the others stopped talking. "I think it shall be in your best interest for the safety of the main island, its ecosystem, inhabitants, human and otherwise, and yourself, Squire Sean, to declare this archipelago an independent, sovereign country. You may then attract some foreign investment and assistance to build a country." Then, Alexandre quickly agreed to apply for A.N. membership as a new country and to request assistance from the Governance Commission to form a provisional government and write a constitution.

"Oh, just what my island needs," Sean raged, "politicians, bureaucrats, contractors, and developers to bulldoze my island and build mansions for rich elitist snobs! And I suppose my immigrants will landscape their manicured front lawns and work in their non-union shops at starvation wages!

"You're not thinking rationally, Sean." Astrid cautioned then rephrased her words after Sean darted a glare at "rationally." "Well rather, logically, pragmatically, or realistically. Sean, the very people you wish to save are for the most part inherently self-destructive and habitually unproductive." She retreated again as Sean, Malika and Alexandre reacted with disapproving glances. "Few possess the necessary skills to develop a functional society to build their own homes and create safe communities with the necessary infrastructure, develop public services, health care, schools, and vocational job training. How will they attract industry, trade, and commerce? We are living light years beyond the prehistoric hunting and gathering age." Malika, her face flushed with anger, moved to confront Astrid, but Alexandre motioned her back. "Were we to somehow provide the skills, knowledge, and tools for them to build, I think we all know how quickly the cities would decay into crime-ridden, drug-infested slums."

Alexandre stepped forward, sternly admonishing her, "That's quite enough colonialism for today, Astrid."

Malika could contain herself no longer. Stepping forward with a steely stare at Astrid, she strained to keep from shouting, her body shaking, she said contemptuously, "Congratulations, Squire Sean, you are to become the proverbial white man's burden."

Chapter Ten

SQUIRE SEAN, THE BENEFACTOR.

—◦◦◦—

"We think sometimes that poverty is only being hungry, naked, and homeless. The poverty of being unwanted, unloved, and uncared for is the greatest poverty. We must start in our own homes to remedy this kind of poverty."

—Mother Teresa.

"The worst poverty isn't about not having enough money to survive. Real poverty is when there is no one in the world who loves you. When there is no other human to make you feel like you matter. As if you aren't worth the air you breathe. Poverty of love is the worst thing you can be deprived of."

—Paige Dearth.

"Seven out of ten Americans are one paycheck away from being homeless."

—Pras Michel.

"Send me your displaced, your dispossessed, your discouraged, your destitute, your disaffected, and your disinfected."

—Squire Sean the Benefactor.

As BERT DAWSON PREDICTED, hordes of land-hungry new age pioneers, desperate immigrants and impoverished settlers were soon bursting at the gates to descend upon the shores of New Atlantica, biting at the bits like thoroughbreds at a racetrack all seeking a better life in a new home of opportunity, promise and freedom from want, abandonment and public scorn and ridicule. To avert the chaos of disruptive land claims and mob violence, Alexandre Begré had finally persuaded his reluctant friend, the former Sean Fidwitter, presently the Marquess of Rutherford or more informally, the self-styled Squire of New Atlantica to accept the informed counsel of the Governance Commission to assist with land management, crowd control, bureaucracy, infrastructure, mass immigration and establishing a provisional government.

"Why did this have to be so damn complicated? I just wanted to give some land to homeless people. Why can't the immigrants police and govern themselves?" Sean grumbled aloud to no one or anyone who might listen before begrudgingly meeting with the Governance Commission, most prominently (as Alexandre described them, the Triarchy) the all-too-familiar and sometimes hostile faces, Professor Anton Gunter-Ellis, General Erich von Schvinghammer, and corrupt corporate raider billionaire J.J. "Jake" Gillis.

Following a relatively mild reprimand by Alexandre, primarily to pacify the righteous indignation of Sean and Malika, Astrid returned to the Sirius yacht along with managing partner Bert to service awaiting clients and assign cases to associates. Astrid would never return to New Atlantica nor speak with Sean again. Likewise, she would remain forever estranged from Malika Bello.

"The only true constant in life is change. Those who fail to adapt are as doomed to extinction as Neanderthals," Alexandre calmly reminded those still present after Astrid's sudden departure. He commented on social evolution and reassured the skeptical staff, saying, "If immigrants need reorientation, education, vocational training, or other resources to succeed here, the Governance Commission will provide the essential tools in line with their mission." Despite some sensitivities being bruised, there was an undeniable truth in Astrid's harsh critique of the unemployed and homeless immigrants. Those who refused to adapt or failed to anticipate technological advances and automation saw their job skills become obsolete and their traditional roles disappear. It's natural to blame "others" for losing once-reliable family trades and professions, especially jobs passed down through generations with minimal training, or lost due to factory shutdowns, layoffs, or retooling. Once marketable skills in labor-intensive industries became inadequate in the face of modern, highly skilled, computer-driven industries. The once-thriving middle class, declining to retrain or hindered by demographics or geography, often through no fault of their own, found themselves unemployed and left in the cold. In frustration and anger, they looked for someone or something to blame. The only true constant in life is change. Those who fail to adapt are as doomed to extinction as Neanderthals," Alexandre calmly reminded those still present after Astrid's sudden departure. He commented on social evolution and reassured the skeptical staff, saying, "If immigrants need reorientation, education, vocational training, or other resources to succeed here, the Governance Commission will provide the essential tools in line with their mission." Despite some sensitivities being bruised, there was an undeniable truth in Astrid's harsh critique of the unemployed and homeless immigrants. Those who refused to adapt or failed to anticipate technological advances and automation saw their job skills become obsolete and their traditional roles disappear. It's natural to blame "others" for losing once-reliable family trades and professions, especially jobs passed down through generations with minimal training, or lost due to factory shutdowns, layoffs, or retooling. Once marketable skills in labor-intensive industries became inadequate in the face of modern, highly skilled, computer-driven industries. The once-thriving middle class, declining to retrain or hindered by demographics or geography, often through no fault of their own, found themselves unemployed and left in the cold. In frustration and anger, they looked for someone or something to blame those who abandoned them, upper management, wealthy elites, the entitled youth, corrupt politicians, radicals, protesters, disloyal consumers, outsourcing, foreign competitors, labor unions, or any perceived perpetrators of what they saw as job theft. This led to xenophobia, racism, bigotry, mob violence, and resentment against the privileged upper classes, fueled by the belief that "they stole our jobs!" e: those who abandoned them, upper management, wealthy elites, the entitled youth, corrupt politicians, radicals, protesters, disloyal consumers, outsourcing, foreign competitors, labor unions, or any perceived perpetrators of what they saw as job theft. This led to xenophobia, racism, bigotry, mob violence, and resentment against the privileged upper classes, fueled by the belief that "they stole our jobs!"

The Governance Commissioners arrived on the island within a month, some of whom, the Triarchy, with their obvious agendas, to establish or enhance personal political, economic, military, or other career-based power bases in the fledgling new country. Select Sirius Law Group staff members (by now a worldwide legal corporation), advisors, diplomats, scholars, seasoned bureaucrats, and technocrats were with Squire Fidwitter at seminars, work groups, and conferences with the numerous commissioners of virtually every field of government. Alexandre, eager to complete the island preparations for the new settlement and return to his lucrative global law practice, volunteered his and young junior partner Malika Bello's services, fearing that the Triarchy might too easily manipulate Sean in island governance negotiations.

Chapter Eleven

NATIONAL DEFENSE: SCHVINGHAMMER.

"Wars are never fought for altruistic reasons."

—Arundhati Roy.

"Nothing so comforts the military mind as the maxim of a great but dead general."

—Barbara W. Tuchman,
The Guns of August.

Malika Bello sat with Sean as his advocate and legal counsel, Alexandre Begré having recused himself from this conference, citing apparent conflicts of interest from his past contentious and litigious history with Schvinghammer.

"*Squire* Fidwitter, you're not getting the cream of the immigrant crop." Schvinghammer ranted. "You're getting the worst of the bunch, the dregs of society, the scum of the Earth! The homeless of the world will swarm onto your island like Biblical crop-destroying locusts."

"How will you know they're even on the island?" Malika taunted him with soft-spoken ridicule. "Aren't the homeless invisible? Don't we ignore them?"

The general paused for a moment, sternly staring at Malika, annoyed at what he considered a full general, a rude, disrespectful interruption.

"The responsible, the ambitious, the well-educated with homes, families, and jobs won't be coming to your island. They will stay where they are. Your beloved homeless, unemployed immigrants are a lazy, angry, desperate lot of violent criminals, alkies, and drug addicts." The general continued to rant, his face red, the veins in his temples bulging. Then, pausing again to regain his composure, he stated more quietly and slightly calmer, "If you don't want mob rule and anarchy, murdering, stealing, looting, and trashing your pristine island, I strongly suggest that you authorize complete military mobilization under my command."

"There'll be no troops. There'll be no mobilization. There will be no standing army! I am not about to tolerate police intimidation and profiling of homeless people, of poor people, or anyone whose race, age, or looks they don't like, not on my island, Hell No!" Sean declared resolutely to Malika's grinning approval.

"How will you maintain order, Squire? It'll be lawlessness, mob rule, vigilantism, sheer anarchy!" the general further pleaded, emphasizing each word.

"Order? I guess I was counting on the honor system, Herr General." Sean shrugged with complacency, then, to Malika's amusement, continued with abject sarcasm, "You do know of honor, don't you, Mon Général?"

"As a military careerist," the insulted general sputtered, "I assure you, Sir, my code of ethics, my honor is inviolable!" Then after a momentary respite, "Begging Your lordship's kind indulgence," Schvinghammer continued emphasizing the royal etiquette with equal sarcasm, "this will be a land rush of chaotic, historic proportions. What's to keep these people," he said derisively," from murdering each other over a slice of dirt, fighting and killing one another for homesteaded soil?"

Malika raised an open palm to cut off the general. She leaned into a whispered huddle with Sean. Then following the hushed consultation, patiently explaining the land allocation plan to the pompous general, "General, under the leadership of Senior Counsel, Alexandre Begré," she began, delighting the general's discomfort by emphasizing the name of his nemesis, "we have already planned for that contingency through the equal distribution of property to all parties; no individuals, family nor group of individuals may acquire more land than any other person. Location will be determined by lottery, with certain lands to be preserved for environmentally friendly business and industry, and public lands, and the public access shoreline. Property and border disputes, land abuse, neighborhood disputes, disturbances and nuisances, obstructed views, shoddy buildings, or fire hazards shall be arbitrated by an impartial ad hoc committee elected by the impacted community.

The general still refused to be denied a military presence on the island. He respectfully offered an alternative option to generate island revenues by leasing lands for the construction of "friendly" nation military bases.

"It wouldn't be friendly here for very goddamn long!" Sean railed at him. "It'd look like a damn alliance! We'd be a target of every-fuckin'-one of the "friendly" nations' enemies and every disgruntled terrorist cell they ever pissed off!"

Malika jumped in to assist her client. "I think what Sean is trying to communicate…"

"I know what the fuck I'm saying!" Sean snapped at her, offended by the interruption.

"Excuse me, Sean, if you will allow me as your legal counsel and advocate." She said calmly as Sean backed off. "The island's neutrality would be immediately discredited, its sovereignty compromised. Other countries and nations would assume at least the appearance of an alliance with one or more foreign powers. And that might well make the island more vulnerable to attack." She summarized Sean's concerns about both standing and a guest army on the island.

1. The island's anti-war ideology
2. unknown cost-benefit analysis

3. The appearance of a favored nation's status

4. The island would become a target of belligerent nations and terrorists

5. The island's neutrality policy would be challenged and questioned internationally, and finally

6. Alexandre Begre's history with the Schvinghammer military family would be problematic.

"What will make this island most vulnerable," the general lectured, "is the complete lack of any military presence on the island."

Sean rose to argue but sat as Malika placed her comforting hand atop his. He turned toward her, his eyes looking at her face affectionately, floating upon her words, enamored by her strength as she calmly but resolutely dismissed the general.

"We shall take your warning under advisement, General. Now, please excuse us as I discuss your recommendations with my client. It is, after all, still *his* island and therefore, under his complete authority.

Then, the general angrily and disgustedly snapped his heels, turned sharply, and exited with displeasure from the room.

Chapter Twelve

GOVERNANCE: GUNTER-ELLIS.

⸺◆⸺

"Caste coalitions will disintegrate in front of good governance."

—Rajnath Singh.

"The human race divides politically into those who want people to be controlled and those who have no such desire."

—Robert A. Heinlein.

ALEXANDRE CONSIDERED AGAIN RECUSING himself from the seminar with "the professor" Anton Gunter-Ellis (AGE) as his former "favorite student" to avoid embarrassing his best friend, Sean, the professor's "worst student." AGE had offered to personally mentor the young shining scholar on several occasions, only to have Begré politely and diplomatically decline each time. Finally, more bluntly and somewhat bitingly, refused the professor's mentorship in part due to AGE's harsh treatment of Sean.

"The academic path to my professional goal is abundantly clear. Should I require any career advice, I shall heed the words of an actual law professor or private barrister rather than those of an undergrad humanities lecturer."

Begré was neither harsher nor blunter to the professor than AGE had been to Begre's hedonistic confidante, compatriot, and, some would shockingly suggest, alter ego, Sean Fidwitter, whom he sincerely believed was completely incompatible and an evil fortune to Begre's scholastic pursuits.

"For the life of me, I cannot even imagine the bizarre circumstances which sanctioned your admission into this exceptional university, but mark my words that I intend to correct this grievous fallacy." AGE cruelly told Sean in front of a packed classroom following one of Sean's hilarious responses that incited uproarious laughter among the other students.

Sean's other professors, his many friends and classmates who delighted and admired his nonchalant demeanor and infectious humor and especially the university's bean counting comptroller strongly disagreed with this assessment. Sean was neither an indolent nor incompetent student but rather a frequently bored one who excelled in those subjects that excited him and barely squeaked by some of the required courses, "this will prepare us for life how?" and disrupted entire classrooms with his loud snoring during interminable lectures, particularly those delivered in monotone by AGE.

"Maybe we should both recuse and pay some poor out-of-work flunky to listen to the professor drone on about Max Weber's Iron Cage." Sean suggested.

"No, that's too cruel—to some poor innocent flunky." Alexandre laughed.

"Well, then let's not miss a golden opportunity to re-torment the bastard." Alexandre nodded. "Mais oui. We will both attend his lecture series and rescue Malika from the tedium."

Malika's pride was wounded. She fervently protested her unfair exclusion—as a junior partner she thought, from this vital session with Dr. Gunter-Ellis, a renowned public administration law and policy scholar. She insisted upon attending every meeting, conference and seminar as Sean's legal advocate and protector lest the commissioners confuse and overwhelm Squire Sean the Benefactor with legalese, bureaucratic acronyms, and technicalities to wrest the control and proprietorship of his island.

Sean was once again offended that Malika felt he needed protection from "those asshole bullies" and that he couldn't "see through their hidden agendas."

"I'm merely looking out for you Sean as a friend and valued client." She assured him.

"What, we're friends?" he looked at her, his head cocked to one side.

She nodded, smiling shyly. Sean blushed, smiling back at her and Alexandre offered a compromise, Malika accepting second chair seated to the right side of Sean—which pleased him immensely-as an interested though quiet observer but at her insistence the right to challenge all or any part of the presentation and to demand clarification of vague talking points.

Alexandre as always served as lead counsel to Sean left so that the best friends might nudge each other whenever one or the other nodded off during the professor's loquacious presentation. Should both begin to snore, Malika was to kick Sean from under the table who would in turn awaken Alexandre.

Anton Gunther-Ellis, the holder of three doctorate degrees had failed Sean in his required courses, put him on academic probation prior to expelling him from the University deeming him "a bright young man but at best a lackadaisical student, only rarely shining scholastically for selected topics of discussion in the classroom when attending but frequently absent and failing to submit required term papers."

Sean could not avoid meeting with "the professor," as the main island's only permanent legal resident and sole registered, legal titled owner. Alexandre the honors graduate and world-renown barrister and his youngest partner Malika Owusu were neither intimidated by the unforgiving, "strict grading" staid college professor. Sean felt even less so as "that lackadaisical student who always seemed to stagger drunkenly into a mountain of cow manure and crawl out of smelling like a perfumed rose."

Anton Gunter-Ellis, one of the sharpest and youngest of any university-level doctorates, was silently floundering like a rudderless ship in a perpetual sea of inertia in his career. Unlike "the laziest sloth of a quasi-student of my entire academic life," AGE lacked Sean Fidwitter's reliable resiliency. The only improbable link of commonality between the two was their sudden irony as the tortured victims of a cruel cackling demonic twist of fate, casting them adrift.

Gunter-Ellis, cold, aloof, and severe, his face antiseptic, his soft monotone voice hopelessly flat without octaves, concealing all passion for any topic, stern and professorial exactly as Sean and Lef recalled him, he droned on endlessly about different government models across the globe, barely making eye contact with either of his two former students, one a dismal failure in his opinion, undeserving of his sudden unearned acquisitions, the other an academic success without equal. He barely noticed Malika, who kept dozing off, waking up whenever her head slipped from her hand propping up her chin or whenever Sean boldly but gently touched her leg with his knee. Eventually, she could no longer feign interest, rose from her seat, and left the room, venturing outside for fresh air.

She returned to the hastily constructed new Education Center's lecture hall to find the professor still orating without pausing for reflection and refreshments, he segued into a long tedious dissertation on government services, with comparative emphasis on capitalism versus socialism, governmental delivery of infrastructure, land management, public utilities, police and fire services, population growth, taxation, wealth distribution and immigration policy.

Eventually between all catnaps, drowsy head nodding, nudges, and hunger pangs, Alexandre convinced the professor to pause for questions, to eliminate the more extreme types of undemocratic government...totalitarianism, military dictatorship, theocracy, communism, oligarchy, and aristocracy by appealing to Sean's egalitarianism, briefly explain governmental models and limit the economic discussion to communism, socialism, and capitalism.

He began with the governmental models each alit on the blank wall and using a laser pointer for his lecture although each attendee reminded the professor that they were well learned with the government types. But he lectured anyway, droning on tediously undeterred until Sean yelled out in complete disrespect.

"Professor, puh-leeze, just give us the fucken highs and lows before your goddamn monotone renders us comatose lingering at Death's door! I know it is covered in class, but my dog ate my notes! Now move on or bugger off!"

Perturbed but cognizant and coveting the opportunity to guide a new nation and establish an international reputation, he capsulized six forms of government that he felt would most interest the incurious Squire Sean. Begré expected to take the lead as the honors graduate, legal scholar, and Squire's counselor. Still, to his and Malika's surprise, Sean seemed well-informed, lucid, sober, and unusually articulate in challenging the professor's arrogance and assumptions of world governments.

DEMOCRACY: "Democracy is the worst form of government—except for all the others that have been tried." Sir Winston Churchill (1874-1965), British Prime Minister (1940-1945, 1951-1955), once stated. Long before the existence of the British Empire, during the Classical period of Ancient Greece, Greek philosopher Plato, sharing Socrates' criticism of Democracy in The Republic, wrote "foolish leaders of Democracy, which is a charming form of government, full of variety and disorder, and dispensing a sort of equality to equals and unequaled alike." Plato had argued, the professor droned, that only a utopian aristocracy led by philosopher-kings, revisited later in Arthurian legend, was the best type of government available in ancient Greece. Athenian democracy, by its anarchic nature, allowed too much freedom to the uneducated, unruly masses, soon degenerating into riotous mob rule, a belief later echoed by American founding father Alexander Hamilton, who argued in favor of an elitist aristocracy as opposed to the Jeffersonian egalitarian expression of participatory democracy.

"Therein lies justification for Burr to kill Hamilton." Sean quipped to Malika and Alexandre.

"Sssh, don't distract the professor from his prepared lecture," cautioned Begré, "lest this agony drag out for months."

"In the interest of brevity," Malika stated, rising partially from her seat like a courtroom attorney, "we will stipulate that except small manageable groups, total democracy is both impractical and inefficient." "Direct Democracy", the professor lamented, "would be a constant state of referendums, gridlocks, endless debates, all resulting in continuous delays in providing public services."

Malika erose again to point out that the antebellum American popular sovereignty policies "codified slavery, legalized grave social and civil injustices, the tyranny of the majority, vigilantism, and the despotism inherent in the rule of the masses."

"We concur with Churchill," Alexandre stated, trying to limit discussion, "that democracy, while flawed in chaotic confusion, was still preferable to the alternatives of fascism, totalitarianism, oligarchies, anarchy, and absolute monarchies."

"We've all read Plato's Republic, Professor," Malika stated, trying to expedite the lecture.

"I don't think I read it," Sean mumbled nearly inaudibly.

"We're going to proceed as if you had," Malika whispered back to him, her hand atop his, comforting him more than flirtatiously. Sean grinned broadly, floating on clouds of romance if not delusion.

"I wonder if I passed the examinations." He asked.

"Mais Oui. You copied my notes." Alexandre humored him.

More prodding from Alexandre urged the professor's brief discussion of other forms of government, with only fleeting disdain for totalitarianism.

Sean, for his part, was in no hurry, content to bask in the warmth of Malika for as many hours as possible.

COMMUNISM: "From each according to his ability, to each according to his needs." Karl Marx had written in Critique of the Gotha Programme (1875), believing that the abundance of goods and services would meet the needs of the population and that no individual would be expected or required to toil beyond his or her capabilities.

More than 100 years earlier, French utopian Étienne-Gabriel Morelly had written in his Code of Nature (1755) that "Sacred and Fundamental Laws" would uproot vice and destroy the evils of a society;"

1. Nothing in society will belong to anyone, either as a personal possession or as capital goods, except the things for which the person has immediate use, for either his needs, his pleasures, or his daily work.

2. Every citizen will be a public man, sustained by, supported by, and occupied at the public expense.

3. Every citizen will make his particular contribution to the activities of the

community according to his capacity, his talent, and his age; it is on this basis that his duties will be determined, in conformity with the distributive laws.

Then, having highlighted the strengths of communism, the professor quickly dismissed existing communist-led countries as State Dictatorships and Oligarchies, which shamelessly enriched the senior party members with homes, dachas, vacations, and luxuries denying the proletariat from power bases, materialistic luxuries and rights and privileges, in effect creating the very class system that Marxism claimed to deplore.

Alexandre stated that a proper communist system acts as a disincentive to individual ambition, achievement, and success, reiterating the familiar criticism of communism. "All things being equal, there is no real incentive for individual achievement, to rise above one's station in life."

"With the government providing all essential services and basic needs, food, shelter, clothing, and health care," Malika said, arguing in favor of socialism, "the individual is relieved of such worries and then free to actively pursue more rewarding goals and dreams."

"This entire discussion would make Jake Gillis cringe." Sean laughed.

"Oh, Gillis would suffer a massive stroke." Alexandre nodded in agreement.

"Mr. Gillis," the professor grumbled scornfully, "is a corporate raiding capitalist."

"A running dog imperialist pig?" Malika joked, mocking the professor.

"A multi-billionaire capitalist pig," Sean added.

"The worst kind of narcissist capitalist, a successful one—without empathy, compassion, or charity," Malika replied.

The professor, feeling he was losing control of his lecture, moved onto what he believed to be, the last two types of government, briefly touching on monarchies both absolute and constitutional and then the elective representative Republic which the professor disparaged hopelessly gridlocked, inefficient, and ineffective handicapped by self-serving agendas and political ambitions of lawmakers, spiteful partisanship, the loyal opposition, catering to ideologues, corrupted by corporate lobbyists and shadow governed by entrenched bureaucracies particularly those locked down in Max Weber's rigid, dehumanized ("next window please, I'm on my break"), stern and unfriendly rule quoting "Iron Cage of social bureaucratization, "the polar night of icy darkness charged with implementing the unspecific policies and programs espoused by politicians for the general welfare and the greater good to make them at least ostensibly workable.

Still, elective representation that clearly differentiated the REPUBLIC form of government from the totalitarianism, military juntas, theocracies, communist state dictatorships, oligarchies, absolute monarchies and elitist cliquish aristocracies remained the most popular form of government even among the most cynical constituents who generally distrusted most politicians and the government itself, devouring convenient flag-waving quasi-patriotic platitudes, pronouncements and talking points with a grain of salt for which the public was almost always over-taxed and underserved.

The professor struggled to compliment Sean as "naively idealistic and humanely well-intentioned, "however, you are describing the fiefdoms of nobles exploiting the labor of the peasants and American Jim Crow sharecropping."

Sean bristled, insulted that he might be thought of as an American Reconstruction Era overseer, a lordship or absentee landlord.

Before Sean or his lawyers could protest, Gunter-Ellis eventually arrived at point, suggesting that Sean form a constitutional monarchy which would reduce Squire Fidwitter to the status of a figurehead, purely ceremonial sovereign, symbolizing continuity and national unity, surrendering all political power and day-to-day governing to an appointed prime minister, non-elected cabinet and quarrelsome, powerless, unproductive and posturing elective legislature body.

To the surprise of his friends, Sean appeared to be mulling over the idea. But then, he summarily dismissed the idea.

"No, I'm not giving any authority as the property owner to sit on a bathroom throne and wear a theatrical costume papier mache crown. Perhaps, I will and modestly continue as the Squire, the kindly landlord assessing user fees rather than burdensome taxes, a cafeteria menu plan allowing the people to prioritize and choose from available public services, revenue sharing, and occasional tributes to defray island management expenses."

"Your compassion for the working class," the condescending professor said with a twinge of sarcasm in his voice, "while praiseworthy is doomed to failure, I would predict, within three years at the most, at which time, I understand, the island as a failed settlement will return to the Duke of Rutherford."

"If you can find him. He's a fugitive, a credit criminal. Good luck with that!" Sean retorted, returning to the professor's sarcasm.

"Sean," Alexandre calmly and quietly advised him, "a cafeteria plan for public and social services is unworkable. It would divert needed revenue and funds from essential services like protective agencies, island defense, government and bureaucratic salaries, and building the infrastructure."

Then Malika gently placed her hand on Sean's shoulder, "Sean, you are giving land to homeless and poor people. They own nothing. They have nothing. They cannot pay for any services at all. You are going to have to create jobs for them. You will need to tax the rich, the developers, and the corporations moving to your island." Sean turned to look at her, gazing into her face as though they were the only two people in a mystical moment, listening to every word, but his eyes locked on her lips. He moved closer to her. This time, she could not help but recognize his unabashed, unfettered attraction for her, withdrew her hand, and slid her chair further away from him.

"Yes?" He prompted her.

"Eh," she stammered nervously, "I've lost my train of thought. I will text my thoughts and concerns to Alexandre later, and he can share them with you." She added, backing away from him.

A saddened, heartbroken Sean rose from his chair as Malika quietly shied away from the table and directed his remarks to the professor. "A constitutional monarchy as opposed to an absolute monarchy in which I retain final and discretionary authority? It's my island until I decree otherwise. Why would I want to be a powerless, meaningless figurehead and political puppet?"

Sean's quiet strength and determination stunned the others. Malika paused by the door, watching in silent curiosity.

"You'd be more than a meaningless, powerless figurehead, Sir, you'd be sovereign, a symbol of patriotic unity." Then the professor warned of absolute authority. "Even among good and noble leaders, the philosopher-king, the potential for tyranny is always present. Remember, Your Lordship, the warning of Lord Acton, "power tends to corrupt and absolute power corrupts absolutely."

Sean quickly countered, quoting Edmund Burke, "The only thing necessary for the triumph of evil is for good men to do nothing.'

Alexandre glanced proudly at his friend Sean as Malika walked toward the table, lingering behind Sean as the young squire continued, "Professor, contrary to your low opinion of me, I am a good man, and I am trying to do something good. This is a philanthropic grant to reduce homelessness and poverty on this planet. We're redistributing the homeless, the poor, the displaced, dispossessed, and despondent peoples who, without this vacant island, would have nowhere else to go."

Malika, impressed by Sean's heroic, altruistic compassion and generosity, returned to the table, standing warmly next to him, arm in arm, beaming proudly at his side. The professor was less impressed and admonished Sean for his unrealistic plan, which he silently considered childish and idiotic.

"You cannot possibly expect to resettle all the homeless, indigent people on this one island. They'd be packed like sardines in a can! They would be cramped together on top of each other. They'd suffocate. Not even you can be so incredibly naive." The professor reproved Sean.

"I'm just giving them some breathing air, elbow room, a warm, dry habitat to stretch their legs out of the rain and the snow, out of the weather and the elements, a little living space!" Sean pleaded.

"The German word for that is Lebensraum." The professor said sternly.

"Living space, Hitler's false justification for invading and annexing more countries and territories for Nazi Germany." Alexandre quietly told Sean.

"I know what the fuck it means! I passed my world history courses!"

Then Malika vigorously objected to the comparative language.

"Professor, if I may, the proposed land grant contains a space available caveat," Alexandre said, rising on behalf of his perpetual client. After exchanging glances, Sean nodded his assent, and Alexandre explained the land grant and immigration program as Sean and Malika resumed their seats, sitting closely together, hands clasped.

But the professor refused to allow the circular debate to die. He insisted on prevailing on behalf of a ruling skilled bureaucracy, a government by technocratic meritocracy. "It's going to be total anarchy without a functioning, solid government with experienced leaders, educated public administrators, and a knowledgeable, highly skilled bureaucracy. These are highly dysfunctional creatures," he said disparagingly, unable to manage their own lives. They lack even the most basic skills to build and operate a fledgling new country!"

"And that is the two-year charter of the Governance Commission to guide the people to construct an egalitarian society, a diversified, robust economy, and a strong central government supported by sovereign provinces and territories."

"Your entire premise of Athenian democracy is built upon a fractured, flawed foundation," the professor persisted. "I see nothing but failure in your future."

"Failure does not rule the day. It is seldom the final word." Alexandre admonished the professor before adding John Fitzgerald Kennedy's Bay of Pigs quote: "Success has a thousand fathers, but failure is an orphan."

Malika felt Sean's right hand clench into a fist, could almost hear his teeth gnash in anger, ready to challenge the professor to parking lot politics, so to avert a physical assault on the professor and subsequent criminal charges against Sean, she rose to end the conference, "Professor, you have lost all your appeal." Malika said curtly. "Class dismissed. You are excused, Sir."

"I think it wise to reschedule your meeting with Jake Gillis," Alexandre suggested after Gunter-Ellis had departed the room, "unless you prefer that we instead meet with him on your behalf."

Then Malika offered to suspend the Gillis meeting indefinitely because of her intense personal hatred for the new age robber baron.

Once again, Sean expressed umbrage that his best friend and romantic interest had so severely underestimated his strength and intelligence. "I can handle Gillis on my own, thank you very much." He said resentfully. "What concerns me more is that two smart barristers cannot see through something so transparent. It's been obvious to me since the very beginning that the commissioners, that this triarchy, Schvinghammer, Gunter-Ellis, and Gillis, are plotting to steal my island from me to rule it together as an oligarchy of three. I'm watching my back. Maybe the two of you should have someone watching yours."

Chapter Thirteen

"YBANIS, GILLIS AND OTHER DECEPTIONS."

"All warfare is based on deception."

—Sun Tzu,
The Art of War.

"Let us never negotiate out of fear. But let us never fear to negotiate."

—John F. Kennedy.

SELDOM IF EVER SINCE Hitler and Stalin agreed to the Non-Aggression Pact in August 1939, were two individuals more opposed in their ideals, ethics, and values and more likely to covertly betray each other than the unprincipled predatory and pragmatic global businessman Jake Gillis and his "easy pickings" prey, the good-natured dogmatic but goldbricking, hedonistic dipsomaniac Sean Fidwitter.

Most people underestimated Sean, close friends, casual acquaintances, educators in childhood as well as college professors, bartenders, barflies, gossips, family members, including his mother, indeed the Duke and Duchess of Rutherford, and even strangers "tripping over me in the dark. "We set the bar very low for Sean Fidwitter." More than a few drinking buddies noted, "And, he has never disappointed us."

If the constant teasing and ridicule hurt him, he never expressed it in any way. He seemed to shrug it off complacently with a smile and ordered another round. Those who occasionally attempted to motivate him, usually through shaming, into some career or vocation to provide him with a steady income, Sean assured him of his goal of one day owning a thriving tavern or pub.

"You go belly up in a year." Advised a chastising friend.

"That was almost too easy. I promise we'll get everything we want from that spineless alky." Gillis later bragged to his cheering colleagues awaiting his return on his luxurious private yacht.

General Schvinghammer and Professor Gunter-Ellis were also in attendance, the general loudly toasting Gillis amid the crowd. The professor, however, watched the celebration from a distance, frowning and skeptical.

Alexandre and Malika were far less festive upon Sean's return. They had worried.

"What a horrid experience!" Sean exclaimed. "I'll never do that again!" They looked at him inquisitively. Then, grinning, he said, "It was pure unadulterated Hell! Never take a meeting with scoundrels, never negotiate when sober."

"We should have taken that meeting for you. Always bring legal counsel to contract negotiations." Alexandre with concern that Sean had given too much away to Gillis. "I warned you not to trust one word spewing out of that *dark money* criminal's devious mouth."

Sean just shrugged off their concerns. Then, Alexandre offered him a drink but to everyone's shock, Sean waved them off. "No, thank you. I'm not thirsty."

"I hope he didn't take unfair advantage of you." Malika said with grave concern.

"No but he thought he did." Sean smiled at her.

Ignoring his lawyers' pleas, earnest warnings, and fervent objections, Sean did agree to meet privately with Jake Gillis at an undisclosed hidden location in the northeast dark and mysterious Ybani Forest under the protection of the mystical but abjectly neutral Ybanis. Unlike the mythical Aquarians, the existence of the towering, fearsome-looking Ybanis had never been doubted; samples of their DNA from hair follicles, urine, and feces had been collected from the soil, analyzed, and verified at the most irrefutably honest scientific laboratories. Scouting parties, anthropologists, and survey teams observing them and capturing their images onto high-definition photo equipment described the Hominidae Ybani, transplanted from jungles unknown, defying detection for eons, as more than seven feet in height, lean yet muscular with chiseled warrior-like features, sunken piercing eyes beneath dark unibrows, and bronze-skinned. They had long been observed and verified by anthropologists and scouting parties but only at the most outer edges of the thick impenetrable forest, usually dawn or dusk, foraging with uncatalogued species of mammals, many resembling deer, elk, canines, felines and smaller pedigrees of horses, donkeys, and alpacas a day feeding time, at daybreak or nightfall. Then, when the feedings were completed or sooner if the observers approached them for a closer look, they would collectively slip back into the impassible forest and vanish from view as the underbrush became entangled with tree trunks, barring entry to all human interlopers, be they curious, friendly, or hostile. Attempts to study and catalogue these bipedal Hominidae, animals, and plant life within this equatorial tropical rainforest were futile; no existing technology could penetrate the dark, dense natural canopies, even by the most powerful space satellites, aerial reconnaissance cameras, or low-flying manned or unmanned aircraft. And finally, for reasons never explained to the public, the A.I. Ecological Science Trusteeship declared the forest "off-limits" and strictly enforced the ironclad rule with armed drones.

Thus, when interpreters and delegates approached the Commissioners and Sean's legal advisers Alexandre Begre' and Malika Bello with the offer from the Ybanis to host and facilitate a private meeting between Commerce and Trade Commissioner Jake Gillis and Squire Sean Fidwitter the parties all reluctantly agreed to the mediation knowing that no one would challenge the imposing stature and unblemished integrity of these forest dwelling Hominidae.

"I'm glad we're excluding the lawyers." Gillis greeted Sean, seated at a small, round wooden table. "Lawyers are shrewd, cunning slime who never negotiate win-win agreements for clients. They're strictly in it for their avarice and greed! I have always negotiated my business deals above board, trusting the honor of a man's word and a firm handshake." He said, extending his open, outstretched hand across the table.

Sean reached the table, firmly accepting Gillis' handshake, then, on the advice of counsel, counted his fingers.

"You don't trust me?" Gillis chuckled, feigning wounded pride.

"Oh, of course I do. Explicitly." Sean smiled with thinly veiled sarcasm. "Every lie spewed, every word spoken truthfully as the tablets chiseled by Moses, minus the spelling errors, of course."

"You must know that your altruism for the deranged, homeless, impoverished masses is not very pragmatic." Gillis counseled in a fatherly tone.

"Poverty is never pragmatic." Sean fired back. "What is pragmatic or even dogmatic about starvation? Poverty is a social injustice."

"They chose that lot for themselves." Gillis countered, guarding his wallet.

"Yeah, right! Abject poverty, exposed to the elements, shivering in the rain, roasting in the heat, scrounging for anything edible, thirsting for acid rain is such an appealing existence. People queue up by the hundreds, thousands, maybe millions just to sign up for poverty, hunger, public ridicule, and the coveted misery of dwelling on the streets in the elements. Oh, I'd buy tickets to that event!"

They glanced at each other, the avaricious capitalist tycoon—who truly thought of himself "a self-made man" after he parlayed his $500 million lottery winnings into a multi-billion-dollar personal empire and, until recently a hedonistic bon vivant, the altruistic fortuitous royal, the commoner noble and somewhere in the private domain of Sean's alcoholic mind, a faint distant voice quietly uttered, "Let the lies begin."

Gillis then reached into the bag, producing a bottle of whiskey and two small drinking glasses. He uncapped the bottle, pouring the whiskey into the glasses, and shoved one to Sean. To his dismay and maybe to Sean's surprise, the offer of a drink was declined.

"You're not drinking?" Gillis asked with surprise.

"I never drink with capitalists, developers, or duplicitous criminals. I try to keep my head clear and my wits about me."

"You don't believe in the free market?"

"I might if it were free."

Gillis leaned closer, studying his mark, then in a suspicious, accusatory tone, demanded, "You talk like a lefty radical, a goddamn commie! What are you, a goddamn fuckin' communist?"

"Not communist, communalist." Sean corrected him.

Undaunted, Gillis continued a cordial, unaggressive demeanor. However, he lingered on the edges of surliness, his hands trembled, and his mouth watered when eyeing the whiskey bottle and the filled glass, testing his resolve.

"A drink might make you more amenable to reason," Gillis muttered.

"I think you mean more pliable to clear-cutting, asphalt, steel, and concrete over-development excavation." Sean hammered away at Gillis. "Then after you've stripped the land of its natural beauty and destroyed Nature's ecological balance, you pack up your heavy equipment, contractors, and crew and disappear, tabulate your profits, and never look back at the damage you've done. You're not paving over my island!" mockingly adding, "Nice work, Gillis, we just love what you've done with the place."

"My island, my island." The stone-faced, disgusted Gillis thought to himself. "Yeah, we'll soon see about that! What makes it your island? Did you create it out of rock, soil, and trees? Did you discover it? Did you conquer it? You cheated a fool, limey duke!" before asking calmly but directly,

"Sean, just how much land does any one man need?"

"How much money does any one man need?" Sean quickly retorted.

"I'm a venture capitalist!" Gillis argued. "I invest most of my profits! I'm a job creator!"

"And I'm sharing the island with those less fortunate, those with nothing. I'm giving most of the land away. I'm only keeping a modest home and small property for myself. The lawyers are already organizing a worldwide land grant lottery for the poorest of the poor. Unlike you and your rich friends, I'm not looking for a return on my investment. It's selfless charity, altruism without reciprocity. So, what's the return on your investment, Jake?

"Your philanthropy must be the best-kept secret ever. Yeah, I know," Sean interrupted with sarcasm, "charity begins at home, your home."

Gillis struggled with his explosive temper, gritting his teeth and moderating the tone of his voice to appear calm. "Your people are not pioneers on the frontier. They don't have the skills to build log cabins and live off land, or they'd be doing it. Those days are long gone." Gillis lectured Sean. "They'll need sturdy homes, cool in the heat, warm in the cold, shelters to keep them dry in wet season and cool in dry season, plumbing and fresh drinking water, fresh edible food, stores and markets, jobs and household incomes, healthcare, and the necessities of life. I can provide that for you at an enormous discount and negligible return on my investment. However," he paused momentarily, then said casually, "if my money and the investments of my associates are somehow too dirty for you, then perhaps you and your green-living, limousine liberals might better seek foreign aid. But, of course, that isn't free, it isn't charity, it's sure the hell ain't no goddamn investment. It comes at crippling cost, a huge return, a national debt you can never repay."

Triumphantly, Gillis poured himself a fresh glass of whiskey, scornfully eyeing Sean, and sat back in his chair. He smirked slightly, never noticing the contemptuous glares of the Ybani observers. Instead, Gillis savored his imagined victory, waiting patiently for Sean's anxious reply. Sean seemed shaken by the exchange. He appeared confused. Leaning forward, his elbows on the tabletop, his chin resting on his trembling hands, eyeing the whole glass of whiskey in front of him. He struggled with the temptation to quench his thirst, to feed his addiction, and steady his nerves. Perspiration ran down the nape of his neck and formed on his forehead like tiny raindrops. The Ybani Honor Guards, unable to interfere with the bargaining negotiations, could watch with compassion. Sean leaned forward, his chin resting in both hands, eyeing the still-filled extra glass of whiskey in front of him. He again shook off the temptation to quench his thirst and steady nerves. He eventually glanced at the Ybani Honor Guards, who sadly shook their heads, concerned, at Sean's trembling body and quivering lower lip. Then, knowingly and violating the unbiased rules of protocol, a guard brought him a glass of fruit juice with a drinking straw. Gillis nervously began to shuffle uncomfortably in his chair. After a moment, the trembling, quivering, and thirst dissipated entirely. The guards smiled kindly and compassionately at Sean, who silently mulled over Gillis's words. Then, with renewed strength and refreshed composure, his blurred eyes clear, his voice strong, he firmly challenged Gillis on the Granito de Ebano mining colony lease.

"I'm going to be completely upfront and honest with you, Gillis as unfamiliar as that is to you. So, prepare yourself for a shock." Gillis sat back, stunned. Sean could barely his own demeanor, the words did not seem to be his own and he felt as if he were only "along for the ride," a mere passenger of his own determined strength. Gillis stirred in his chair, defensively but unable to speak. "The first thing I plan to do is to terminate your lease and shut down your Granito de ebano slave labor mining camp! I'm going to free all its prisoners and repatriate them to the main island here or to their native lands or anywhere else they freely choose to live. And if any wish to remain on that black granite rock, so be it, but they will do so reaping all the rewards of their labor." Sean concluded, his eyes narrowed fearlessly, pointing a threatening finger at the astonished corporate raider.

"You can't do that!" argued Gillis, defiantly.

"*Yes, I can, and I will.*" Sean replied, even stronger. "*This is exclusively my island, the main island, all the perimeter islands, the little islets, and the boulder you call Granito de ebano. I'm breaking the lease, freeing the imprisoned work camp slaves, and shutting you down, Gillis!*"

"Squire Sean," Gillis spoke with cordial familiarity but a scintilla of respect. "It's neither a rock nor a boulder. It's an island, a rocky terrain without soil, no plants, vegetation, fruits, or meat all of which my people air drop to them monthly. They're called "moles" because they—for reasons unknown to us outsiders—live underground of their own volition."

"*I find this hard to believe.*" Sean said with skepticism.

"I'm not surprised by that. I am not offended either, Squire but it's all true." Gillis continued then leaned forward speaking softly in near whisper out of hearing of the Ybanis. "Just between us, I am about to reveal a very closely guarded secret."

"Like your anonymous acts of charity and unlimited selfless philanthropy?"

"It is indeed a mining colony, but it is not a prison work camp, and the miners are not slave labor. That entire pile of rocks,

Granito de ebano, the boulder as you call it, is a clever ruse, a distraction. You can't grow anything there; it's a solid rock of black granite. The miners are very well compensated through generous bonuses, profit sharing, and dividends. They don't wish to leave Isla de Granito de Ebano, but it must be kept a secret. Otherwise, the island would soon be flooded by hordes of murderous thieves and claim-jumping treasure hunters from all over the planet. It would be worse than the mass hysteria of the gold rushes and oil discoveries of the last few centuries. The mineral rights would be contested by the shadiest, shrewdest shysters and upheld by bribed judges in the most civil courts. The miners would be cheated out of every ounce of ore they've ever dug, every penny they've earned, and then tossed into the treacherous ocean currents by marauding bands of bloodthirsty modern-day pirates, the most vicious thugs imaginable."

Sean remained unconvinced. "And, you are their brave heroic protector, the miners another of your private anonymous charities."

Gillis nodded. "Oh, I receive a decent return on my investment. I am not greedy. I do not take unfair advantage of the mine workers."

"Still another well-guarded secret." An exasperated Sean proclaimed, throwing his hands into the air with exaggerated utterance.

"You'll receive a substantial contribution, a bold monetary tribute and sizable increase when we negotiate the new lease. We are mining very precious gems and minerals over there. It's top-secret Squire, even the miners don't know what we're really doing there because the underground facilities and labs are so restrictive, concealed and protected that insects can't crawl inside but if you are willing to work with us…"

"Oh, top-secret, covert mission, mining black granite for what, counter tops?" Sean snickered, sarcastically. "That boulder over there must be crawling with spies, MI-6, CIA, KGB, Germany's FIS, China's MSS, and Mossad. It must be spook gridlock! Seriously, Gillis, you're mining fucking black granite!"

"Graphite!" Gillis blurted out, his hand covering his mouth to keep the Ybanis from hearing his words. Sean shrugged, unimpressed. Gillis leaned closer. "On that inaccessible, guarded rock island right across the Darwin Straits from you and your shyster friends, my people, all with the highest-level security clearances, all of them genius scientists, physicists, chemists, engineers, and technologists in the most secure underground labs, are crystallizing carbon atoms using hyperthermic atom colliders to convert graphite to diamonds. So, you see, those fuckin' miners don't wish to escape or be rescued. Most are goddamn fuckin' millionaires."

Sean burst into laughter. "Of course, how many of us envy the lives of slugs, moles, and gophers? And I did once read a science magazine while sitting upon the bathroom throne of the hyperthermal process that converts graphite to diamonds. It requires a lot of patience, Gillis. It only requires two or three billion years. If you're not pressed for time, I guess you can sit here and wait."

Sean rose to walk away from the table, laughing, muttering, "Black granite, graphite-based diamonds. Anything to hang onto your mining rights, to keep me from breaking your sham lease. Oh, please, Jake." He laughed. "Should you happen to see Sasquatch swimming by atop Nessie or Yeti mounted on unicorns, you might wish to keep that information to yourself."

Gillis was burning with resentful anger as he rose from the table to call after Sean. "Wait! Do you think I'm trying to scam you, sell you a Ponzi scheme, toll bridge, or swamp land in some upscale retirement village?"

"No, snake oil and a pipe dream." Sean taunted him.

Gillis grabbed his arm, whispering. "Wait! I was skeptical too, so my fellow one percenter friends and I have a contingency plan." Sean paused, looking back at Gillis curiously, who beckoned him and said barely above a whisper, extraterrestrial diamonds, each diamond valued in the millions unless some moron gets greedy and floods the market, devaluating the diamonds, as worthless as gravel."

Sean considered the contingency. Astronomers, physicists, and privately funded rocketeers had disclosed for several years that diamonds explicitly rain on Jupiter and Saturn and, quite possibly, Uranus and Neptune due to the massive planets' size, intense gravity, heat, and pressure. Sean did not challenge Gillis on this point. There had been news reports of extraterrestrial diamonds being sold at exorbitant prices on Earth. However, he would not engage Gillis further, knowing of the character and ethics of corporate raiders, entrepreneurs, and tycoons of Gillis' ilk. But he could not envision Gillis sharing his good fortune and astronomical wealth without exacting power, influence, and excessive financial gain for himself. Nor did he wish to dismiss Gillis's value as a patron and investor of New Atlantica out of hand. Gillis was correct, the immigrating settlers were not the pioneers of the Discovery Age and New Atlantica, the unknown frontier. "We should be talking about a diamond-based currency for your new country." Sean nodded. "We'll revisit the terms of the lease with our lawyers."

A more confident Sean Fidwitter, Squire of New Atlantica and Marquess of Rutherford, emerged from the meeting to be escorted safely to the edge of the forest by a squad of elite Honor Guard, their commander presenting Sean with a gift, several months' supply of Ybani "fruit juice."

Chapter Fourteen

SOVEREIGN, PRINCESS, ROYAL COURTSHIP and STORM CLOUDS.

━━◆◆◆━━

"Greatness Evades Most, Teases Many, Embraces Few."

—Author.

"There can never be a king in a free country of honourable people! Monarch, Kaiser, emperor, dictator, Caesar, or shah, they all belong to the submissive and weak-minded societies!"

—Mehmet Murat ildan

"When the legislative and executive powers are united in the same person, or the same body of magistrates, there can be no liberty; because apprehensions may arise, lest the same monarch or senate should enact tyrannical laws, to execute them in a tyrannical manner."

—Montesquieu

"...I'd make a good king. I'm such a regal type."

—Sean Fidwitter.

Findings and Recommendations:

S EVERAL WEEKS AFTER THE on-island conferences, workshops, and seminars wound down, the Governance Commission, having completed its needs assessment, began the monumental task of issuing specialty lottery certificates that were issued internationally to the poorest-of-the-poor, systematically awarding land grants to carefully vetted and diverse groups of indigent peoples from all the habitable continents. The ANTF began the daunting undertaking of transporting millions of displaced, dispossessed, and desperate individuals, families, and entire communities to the small perimeter islands, islets, and outer banks upon naval troop carriers, freighters, cargo ships, and passenger ocean liners in route to their new homeland among the equatorial Atlantic doldrums. Most recipients were excitedly "biting at the bit" at the prospect of new homes built for them by international benefactors at no cost and the free land grants, public services, healthcare, vocational and career training, and tuition-free public education on an uninhabited, unspoiled island, an opportunity almost too good to be true. Sadly, although not surprisingly, many sold, traded, or gifted their certificates of title, frightened by the outrageous conspiracies disseminated by the abusive worst-of-the-worst immoral exploiters of cheap labor, their workforce steadily decreased, fleeing their dire, depressing workstations for the piers and docks, boarding the disembarking ships to New Atlantica. "Socialism!" screamed disgruntled ultra-conservative pundits and politicians as the ranks of untrained, lowly paid employees steadily dwindled, their supervisors, managers, and sweat shop owners struggled with monotonous tasks of menial labor. Those few "loyal" employees who remained almost immediately organized labor unions, grievance committees, threatened walkouts, staged sit-down strikes, formed picket lines, and took a hard line in labor bargaining.

The proposal.

Leading Schvinghammer, Gillis, and a small delegation of A.N. governance commissioners into the lobby, Professor Anton Gunter-Ellis arrived at the recently constructed interim government office building to present their findings and recommendations to New Atlantica's Squire Sean (his preferred form of address over the ostentatious title of royal lineage, Marquess of Rutherford) and his two primary legal advisers, Alexandre Begre and Malika Bello. Only after an over-dressed, officious, and pompous door attendant had formally announced that they did Sean graciously receive them. Then, following the obligatory group bow of diplomatic protocol, Anton Gunter-Ellis (AGE) as chief commissioner finally approached the squire humbly—clearly at some higher-up's insistence-with hat-in-hand personally to report their findings and recommendations resulting from the six-month study of the island's essential needs to gain recognition as a member country of the Alliance of Nations (A.N.).

"Your lordship," he began, nearly choking on the respectful form of address, "with the consensus of the commission, I wish to propose…"

"Uh oh, here it comes," Alexandre muttered to Malika.

"Professor, I'm very flattered," Sean smirked, "but we do not have enough in common for a successful union."

"Warned you," Alexandre whispered to the smiling, nodding Malika.

Ignoring the levity, the professor gulped his disdain, continuing as if uninterrupted. "What the commission is recommending, squire," he said, abandoning references to nobility, "is a provisional government, a quasi-monarchy with the sovereign retaining certain discretionary powers as head of state and a prime minister and cabinet managing a bureaucratic government."

While Sean quietly considered the offer, Alexandre and Malika stepped forward to question the professor.

"There's no parliament, no congress, no legislative or representative body?" Alexandre inquired.

"I did say provisional government, counsellor. A temporary government," age reminded him, brusquely and impatiently, "until such time that the permanent adult population is sufficiently large, educated, and competent to write and ratify a constitution, form a democratic republic, and elect a representative legislature."

"That's elitist aristocracy, you are recommending, not a democracy, not a republic, but an oligarchy!" Alexandre shouted as Sean watched, enjoying the debate in silent amusement. Sean allowed his lawyers to argue on his behalf as he wandered the room, seeming disinterested.

"Who deems when the people are ready to govern themselves, you, professor?" Malika challenged him.

"Self-government is a learning curve, a process, young lady. It takes time. These people will have to wait and be patient."

"Young lady?" Malika winced, offended.

"What did you say about a monarchy, professor?" Sean finally asked, breaking his silence.

Knowing of Sean's venomous public rants against existing monarchies, most notably in the British Isles, his well-known vitriolic hatred of royalty in general, and his resentment specifically toward his "illegitimate father," the errant, deadbeat duke of Rutherford, everyone turned and gawked in surprise.

"But you abhor the monarchy! You deplore all monarchies." Alexandre reminded him.

"Let us not be too hasty here, let us not rush to judgment." Sean taunted them. "No, I abhor that monarchy; I deplore those monarchies. This one has great promise."

"You scheming little hypocrite!" Malika laughed. "You conniving fraud!"

"I'd make a good king. I'm such a regal type."

"He's fuckin' serious," Alexandre said in shock, turning to Malika.

"Shall we begin the preparations for your coronation, your damned highness?" Malika taunted him with sarcasm.

"Your Royal damned Highness." Sean flippantly corrected her. "It'll be a modest, simple affair," Sean smiled, almost self-mockingly, "semi-formal, of course, by invitation only with just the immediate family and a few close friends."

"There are those born to greatness, others to whom greatness beckons and from time to time permits fools to stumble over it in the dark." The professor grumbled to the other commissioners as they exited the room, leaving the two dismayed lawyers to elucidate the varying monarchies to their regal friend, "and may the world take pity on us all."

A Quasi-Constitutional Monarch.

"Every man is guilty of all the good he did not do."

—Voltaire

Sean demonstrated little taste for power and none for ostentatious glitz and glamor. "I decree that there shall be no pompous, royal pageantry, bejeweled crown, gaudy regal garments, precious metal orb, diamond-encrusted sceptre or sword. And I am not to live in a palace, I dwell in a house, the more rustic, the better." Sean declared to Alexandre, Malika, and a coterie of advisers three months later, just weeks before the coronation ceremony. The event planners and certainly the conniving triarchy of Gunter-Ellis, Schvinghammer, and Gillis were aghast at the "pretensions of commonality." His trusted counselors and confidantes, Alexandre and Malika, on the other hand, were exceedingly pleased and felt that the immigrant masses would be impressed—even reassured-by Sean's populist gesture of humility.

The coronation committee members, recruited explicitly for flawlessly choreographing elegant society balls, celebrity galas, inaugurals, and lavish royal coronations, not surprisingly strongly objected, complaining that the egalitarian, unrestricted event would demean royalty.

"*That* is precisely my intention." Sean concurred.

The emerging, plotting triarchy, Gunter-Ellis, Schvinghammer, and Gillis, although invited to view the coronation along with all the other commissioners and seated among the "great unwashed" immigrants, vagabonds, stragglers, and squatters, were all incensed that none of them had been asked, approached, or vetted to sit in the fledgling new government.

The professor had openly lobbied the king and his councilors, asking that they appoint him prime minister. The king, without rancor, politely refused. He soon found himself exiled to the political wilderness. He earned a modest income as a visiting lecturer, author, and public administration consultant. Eventually they wed a much younger though socially poised, scholarly teaching assistant, Amy (Amelia) Logan, formerly of Canberra, Australia, they traveled the globe for more than a decade, selling the professor's public policy advice to undeveloped nations and emerging countries for a nominal fee, food and lodging while attempting to resurrect his academic reputation.

Schvinghammer fully expected to organize and command the armed forces and was promoted to Field Marshal but claimed that he had once more slighted and betrayed by the intrigue and jealousy of unappreciative policy-making professional bureaucrats, then deactivated by ANTF and retired to civilian life. As a lobbyist and consultant to global defense contractors, he earned a lucrative living and comforted his family with extended absences from home.

Jake Gillis still hungered for power, but unlike the professor and the general, the shady investor, unscrupulous financier, and ruthless corporate raider, Gillis entertained no aspirations for public office. He had angled for Chancellor of the Exchequer (US Secretary of the Treasury) until informed of the requirement to place his vast financial holdings in "blind trust" to avoid a conflict of interest. He chose instead to offer his services as "royal fiscal adviser" sans compensation.

Contrary to the commissioners and others seeking to leave New Atlantica and return to home to their respective native lands, Jake Gillis immediately applied for permanent residency and, after renouncing his U.S. citizenship, almost always seen as an unnatural, unpatriotic act to most Americans, he ordered his corporate offices relocated to the main island, shamelessly bribed bureaucrats and officials, contracted with architects to erect an obtrusive, expansive manor without bothering with building permits and became the island kingdom's most prosperous and one of its most prominent citizens-at least until decades later when incorruptible office holders caught wind of his thievery, the general population became shockingly aware of the scoundrel's malfeasance and sought his arrest and conviction.

The Commoner King and the Detention of Barristers.

"Life is a tragedy for those who feel and a comedy for those who think."

—Jean De La Bruyere.

"There never was a throne which did not represent a crime. The institution of royalty in any form is an insult to the human race. Let us take the present male sovereigns of the earth—and strip them naked."

—Mark Twain.

By the end of the monarchy's second year, the official coronation ceremony was held in the Capitol Pavilion. While the king's humble residence remained in the Northern province, Sean had agreed to locate the capital in the central part of the main island in the province of Capitola. Guests varied with regular citizens attended the Grand Ball alongside world leaders, diplomats, international celebrities, prominent scientists, writers, and humanitarians, the guest list like the land grant drawn at the king's insistence, by lottery. The king also insisted upon "casual dress" for the event and that "gifts, accolades, and tributes to the monarch be strictly omitted." Citing an old proverb, "Beware of Greeks (or any fuckin' one else, he amended) Bearing *Gifts*," the king also declared that anyone violating his order was turned away at the door, promptly escorted off the Capitol grounds, and removed from future guest lists. The offender or offenders' "seat at the proverbial table," Sean stipulated, would be immediately offered to "the most common person(s) available." By the following day, media journalists, social arbiters, and commentators the world over lauded—some bitterly sarcastic-Sean, "the most democratic sovereign ever known to history," naming him "the commoner king." Sean readily and gleefully accepted the moniker and had commoner king embroidered on all his stationery and clothing labels.

"He has his crown, now; he has his country, millions of eternally grateful, friendly subjects..." Malika reminded Alexandre in the waning hours of a diplomatic reception one evening in the not-too-distant future.

"With a stable government now in place," Alexandre noted to Malika, "we may finally soon escape this dreadful isolation and return to the Law."

So finally, after serving as legal consultants to first, Squire Sean the Benefactor and then to the Commoner King, Sean I of the House of Rutherford, Greater New Atlantica's sovereign and constitutional monarch, prepared to leave the island and resume their prominent international law careers. Also, troubling were the circulating rumors of a contentious corporate power struggle between managing partner Bertram Dawson and fiduciary advisor/partner Astrid Nilsson, with depreciating assets and the desertion of wealthy celebrity clients to rival law firms as collateral damage.

But the king, ever conscious of his popularity with his formerly destitute, degraded subjects, feared their untimely departure might prove perilous to the stability of his government of grim, dispassionate bureaucrats and colorless, unimaginative administrators.

"Nay, nay, I say! By order of his Majesty the King," Sean joked as he bounded up behind the two lawyers from across the dance floor, sloshing and spilling a Ybani fruit juice. "Thou shalt not, shalt not, abandon thy sovereign to miserable fates, ambitious evildoers, malicious plotters, and a political destiny most foul! No one, absolutely no one, leaves this island without the express permission of the King. Now, we shall speak of this no more."

"Your Majesty," Malika laughed. "We are not your subjects!"

"Merely non-residents without visitor visas." Said Alexandre, joining in the mirth. "Free to leave at will. We are not even immigrants, we are lawyers."

"Lawyers!" Sean gasped, mockingly. "Trespassers, interlopers, gate-crashing barristers! Guards! Guards!" he shouted in fun to alarmed sentries. "Arrest them! Take them in the tower, off with their heads, off with their heads!"

Then, grinning, Sean turned and returned to the ballroom, mingling comically with the guests, acting for his guests, most of whom were formerly homeless, impoverished, barely clothed, and starving.

"You know," Alexandre smiled, turning to Malika as the novice ruler vanished into the crowd of celebrating guests, "I think he preferred him before he was sober; the Ybanis cured his alcohol addiction."

Malika objected. "Exception. I don't concur."

Looking knowingly at Malika, Alexandre reassured her, "I suppose we could…" he paused, "remain here a tad longer."

Nodding, Malika smiled slightly.

The lawyers agreed to remain on the island for another two years as the king's legal advisors and his First (Alexandre) and Second (Malika) Councilors.

Within weeks following the coronation grand ball, and without consulting Astrid, Bert, or any of the other partners, Alexandre, arbitrarily promoted Malika to the senior partner and Chief Operating Officer of the Sirius Law Group by-passing the seniority and loyalty of Bert and Astrid, with the understanding that she has full decision-making authority in Alexandre's, the founder and Chief Executive Officer, absent. Then, as reports of declining assets and boardroom squabbles dwindled to the island, Alexandre and Malika agreed to alternate trips to Sirius New York and London headquarters every three months to monitor corporate policy, decisions, review caseloads, and mediate personal conflicts.

In the meanwhile, Sean's romantic feelings for Malika grew exponentially daily, although he was always a respectful gentleman, practicing forbearance, never approaching her aggressively or inappropriately. Despite her genuine affection for Sean's impressive maturity, admiration as a compassionate monarch, and his continuous sobriety, her feelings remained locked inside her heart. Her flirtatious lapses were limited to ambiguous smiles and an occasional embrace in friendship, always out of sight of the king's court and gossip.

Interlude: Consort Queen.

"We don't foresee an heir for you, future birthright claims, nor the hereditary line continuing unless you find a suitable queen consort." Advised the Ybani ambassador to the Court of Sean I.

"We see darkness looming, clouds of doom above, and evil lurking in every corner." Counselled the court mystic.

The protocol adviser then interjected, "The king cannot simply date like the rest of us, Your Majesty."

"I don't see why the hell not." Sean snapped. "I *am* the goddamned king. I ought to have some rights." He grumbled. Then he quietly downplayed their worries. "If the ambassador and my court jesters," he said sarcastically, "will all give me some privacy, I do have someone in mind."

Once alone, Sean sighed deeply and summoned his courage.

"I don't share the passion or depth of your feelings." Malika gently told Sean, declining Sean's third and final marriage proposal.

"You could be Queen." He told her.

"I am a queen." She said confidently. "Nothing can take away the affection of friendship I feel for you." She assured him.

Sean was silently devastated but nodded his quiet understanding. "I hope it won't be awkward for you to remain in my employ."

Malika nodded sweetly. "I shall remain her as your friend and as Second Councilor so long as my services are of value to you."

Choking back his tearful emotions with one of his most infrequent royal waves, he excused her. Although she knew how much formality and royal protocol annoyed him, she curtsied slightly before she departed the king's office to meet with the awaiting nominees to the High Court.

The Princess, Lucia De La Mer.

As soon as Alexandre returned from global conferences on the king's behalf, Sean, still nursing rejection and a broken heart, invited him to his humble bungalow overlooking the Darwin Straits.

Expecting that his longtime friend desired to "pour out his broken heart" while abandoning his sobriety, Alexandre was surprised to find Sean sober, elegantly dressed as a king and in high spirits. Hardly despondent from his recent unrequited ardor, he seemed almost buoyant in the company of an exotic olive-skinned, exquisitely athletic young woman with sunken cheeks and long jet-black hair flowing over her shoulders. Her dark, hypnotic eyes beckoned the long-term career-oriented bachelor, Alexandre, to an unfamiliar romantic atmosphere. His gaze was drawn further by her long, fluttering eyelashes, which complemented her arched, dark eyebrows. Elegantly dressed in a long purple evening gown with a single slit revealing a long, dark, shimmering, smooth leg, her polished white teeth sparkled as her full red lips parted, her friendly smile greeting Alexandre into the parlor. Alexandre paused momentarily to regain his composure, his equilibrium, and ever-confident demeanor, then smiled, bowing courteously before gliding in his usual charismatic style toward the king and his stunning guest, chivalrously offering her his hand.

"Lucia," said Sean, offering introductions, "allow me to present my dear friend, lawyer and First Counselor Alexandre Begre."

Lucia smiled politely, her voice smooth and appealing, "Of course, your legal reputation and fame precede you, kind sir."

"Lef," Sean said with subdued geniality, "My cousin, Her Royal Highness, the Princess Lucia de la Mer, who favors us with an extended royal visit."

"De la Mer?" Alexandre mused, immediately recognizing the French language words. "Lucia, of the sea?"

Lucia smiled playfully. "Bien sûr." (FR. Of course, certainly). "And Alexandre?" Does that not translate to the Source? Is that sheer arrogance or hubris, Monsieur? And what of Begre,' Is it Be-gree or Beggar?"

Alexandre wondered if he had finally found his match in the princess's engaging repartee. Embarrassed and speechless, he looked to Sean to rescue him. But Sean was enjoying the banter. Princess Lucia was proving herself a relentless and charming challenge to the indefatigable courtroom debater, and Sean was hesitant to end it. Eventually, he did take mercy on his friend.

"Oh, what's in a name? Both of you should be grateful that you were never saddled with Sean Fidwitter."

"Oh, my sweet cousin, Sean, ever the gallant rescuer, still breaking the tension with self-effacing humor." The princess laughed.

"Magnifique, Mon Ami. You found your family." Alexandre congratulated Sean.

"They found me." Sean replied evasively.

"Cousin to a princess, a royal princess. How ironic for a vociferous anti-monarchist." Alexandre the barrister probed. "Of royal lineage. But certainly not in your mother's line, Crystal Chandelier, the exotic dancer."

"Pole dancer." Sean corrected him without guilt or shame.

"Not the Rutherford line, either." Alexandre continued the query. "The settlement required a non-disclosure agreement barring you from further investigating the duke's lineage and paternity."

"Why the sudden interest in my genealogy?" Sean snapped. "Stop acting like a fuckin' inquisitor!"

"I cannot help myself. I am a fuckin' lawyer, goddamn it." Alexandre countered.

"Distant cousins." The princess interceded.

"Very distant, extremely far away," Sean said, trying to veer Alexandre away from the query. "I am amazed she found me."

"It required tireless research, Cousin," Lucia said, emphasizing their relationship. "Our common ancestor was difficult to trace. It was an exceptionally long time ago, centuries!"

"Yes, well, just water under the bridge, as they say." Sean quipped a bit, revealing himself before excusing himself to leave

Alexandre and Lucia alone together in the parlor. "I am delighted you are here, my most regal cousin, Princess. But I am still the King." He told her. "I do have royal duties to perform." Turning to Alexandre, he commanded, "My First Councilor, Monsieur Alexandre Begre', Esquire, shall be pleased to serve as your guide around the island. I promise that he will protect you to his last breath of life." Then, before Alexandre or Lucia could protest, the king turned sharply and exited the room.

Royal Gossip and Romance.

In the weeks that followed, Alexandre and Princess Lucia were inseparable. They were seen everywhere together to the delight of the royal gossips, paparazzi, and their public, both admirers and detractors.

And one night, they attended the grand opening of a contemporary dance club with King Sean and Second Councilor Malika Bello charming the many guests with their informal sociability, friendliness, and congeniality. The next day, royal publicists, entertainment reporters and general gossips made note of the king and his Ebonese girlfriend (a comment that irritated the very private Malika for at least two reasons and annoyed the empathetic Sean, knowing Malika did not wish to be known as 'the king's girlfriend," only as his Second Councilor, attorney, and casual friend) danced with any and every guest who asked them. Although they tried their best to convince all that they were "just friends," incurable romantics swooned and left the dance floor whenever Sean and Malika took to the dance floor, waltzing in each other's arms as the band leader selected a special "love song" for them. Finally, when the music faded at the end of their last romantic waltz, with their arms around each other and Malika's head resting on his shoulder, Sean whispered apologetically. "I'm sorry, Malika. I only wanted to go dancing together. I honestly expected the focus to be on Alexandre and Lucia. I fear the gossipy talk will be all about us as a…"—he stammered before blurting out, "a romantic couple in love. I will issue a complete denial tomorrow morning."

"To no avail." She smiled sweetly. "No matter how strenuous our denials, they'll never be convinced."

"I'm the King. They're my subjects." He said softly, in jest. "They'll believe whatever I tell them, or I'll banish the lot of them." Then, more seriously, he shrugged like an innocent little boy. "Don't worry, I'll broadcast a royal speech. Shall I do that, Malika?"

Malika smiled, thinking any official denials by this time to be futile and unbelievable, or with a change of heart and not minding the public attention as much as she thought, looked lovingly up at him, slipped her arms around his neck, and told him, "Shut up and kiss me."

They embraced tightly, their lips pressed together to the sheer delight of the crowd, who cooed, cheered, and applauded, all but Alexandre and the Princess standing together watching from a darkened corner, their arms around each other, both looking quite surprised.

"It appears that their amour is no longer a secret," Alexandre commented.

The princess laughed. "We've been upstaged."

A Royal Courtship.

In the idyllic months that followed, away from the clamor of the enamored crowds, incessant royal watchers, and snooping gossip reporters all currently distracted by King Sean's highly publicized "orchestrated, pretend" romance with Second Councilor Malika Bello, First Councilor Alexandre was free to discreetly court Princess Lucia—and she him—out of the public eye in relative privacy and enjoy their time alone together. He was suspicious that his introduction to the beautiful, glamorous, and Greek goddess-like "princess cousin" might well be still another ploy to keep both he and Malika on the island lest they abandon the companion-starved king by returning to their law practice "on the Continent," in the Americas, the World Court, and other world capitals.

Yet, Alexandre was thoroughly entranced by Lucia and did not struggle, protest, or resist her "hypnotic, dream-like spell over him," his first-ever serious infatuation that rendered even his illustrious legal career seem trite and tiresome by comparison.

Soon the couple was regularly embarking on almost daily dry season strolls along the four shorelines, clearly enthralled with each other, falling or diving in passionate and undeniable love with one another, traveling to all parts of the immense island seemingly "in the blink of an eye" and almost "miraculously" evading the incessant paparazzi, jealous members of the king's court, provisional government spies and virtually all onlookers but occasional fishermen, beachcombers, seasonal swimmers, fearless surfers, and scattered sunbathers.

As they frolicked on the dunes together one warm day, the incisive courtroom barrister gave in finally to his inquisitive nature, trying to learn more of the princess's sketchy background, untraceable family history, dubious relationship to her *distant cousin Sean,* and, most importantly, her identity.

"You are an enigma, Princess, a woman without a verifiable past from places unknown, unrevealed parentage, and obscure ancestry." Alexandre probed hesitantly with deliberate non-accusatory caution.

"We should all be mysteriously exotic and unfamiliar rather than mundane mediocrities, such tedium." She said, evasively, with a seductive smile. "How important is this to you, now? Are you my suitor or my inquisitor?"

"I don't know who you are." He pressed further.

"You will know everything in time."

"And when do you think that time might be?" He inquired softly.

"I expect," she answered with a slight smile, "at the altar." Then she leaned forward and kissed him.

On whatever shoreline they visited, the typically exacting lawyer and his exotic princess could not help noticing the scarcity of other people on the beaches. Lucia did eventually comment on that as well as the ever-presence "voyeurs" watching them through telescopic lenses from the man-made dunes, noting the improbability of drifting sands forming natural dunes in the windless, calm doldrums.

Almost daily throughout the dry season, they relished the privacy of the abandoned beaches well away from the more urban crowds, allowing them the blissful opportunity to become more intimate despite the ever-present, watchful bodyguards, possibly reporting their movements to the fledgling provisional federal government, the princess suspected. Begre's suspicions were cast on "an even more corrupt entity than government, the 'dummy' corporations, shell companies, and concealed conglomerates all under Jake Gillis sleight of hand."

"I have been unable to discover why your cousin would grant Gillis untethered freedom from governmental oversight and environmental regulations. This is so atypical of Sean the Benefactor."

"They cleared the beaches and drove everyone off the shoreline? I assumed that our sentimental Sean wished us privacy to embolden our budding romance."

Alexandre shook his head, "Sean would be outraged if he knew of this. He has a temper that I don't desire provoked until the investigation develops a prima face case. The shorelines, beaches, inland waterways, and recreational areas are all part of the King's Public Lands Access Decree."

"What possible interest would this Jake Gillis have in our sojourns, secluded hideaways, and romantic getaways? Why would he protect our privacy or keep the curiosity-seekers from interrupting our time together?" she asked curiously.

"Simply, Princess, to keep me away from the King, to isolate him from the conservationists, industry regulators, and environmentalists."

"How could Sean be so blind? Why would he allow this?"

"Altruism. Gillis agreed to create gainful employment for the immigrants and general populace, and the king agreed to look the other way -for the time being."

The princess looked genuinely concerned. "How long will you allow this to continue?"

"Until it can be tolerated no longer."

The Chess Metaphor.

"So many royal watchers, paparazzi, and voyeurs." Malika sighed forlornly, peering out through the northern view bay window of the king's residence at the daily

assembled throngs of curiosity-seeking royal
watchers, reporters, voyeuristic sycophants,
hangers-on, wannabes, and obsessive celebrity
junkies. She pulled the drapes closed and,
looking bored with the entire ordeal, drifted
back to the chess table.

"You're not a prisoner. This is all a
diversion. You agreed to this charade. You're
free to leave anytime." Sean said calmly,
without looking up, as he assembled the
chess pieces on the board for a new match.

"Oh please, Your Majesty," she groaned,
sitting across from him.

"White or black?" Interrupted her. She
glared back at him. "Oh, naturally, black."
He answered himself, rotating the board,
black pieces to her.

"White moves first." She reminded him.

"Not on my island," Sean told her. "I'm
an equal opportunity sovereign."

"You know I can't so much as step outside
without being mobbed."

Sean shrugged. "You could get off the
island under the cover of darkness in one
of the planes here in my private airport.
You can go anytime."

"That is not the impression that Alexandre
and I have."

"Then you both impulsively jumped to
conclusions. I over-reacted to renewed
fears of abandonment. I promise that the
next time I lose my temper, I am not even
going to look for it. Whoever finds it
can keep it." He mumbled. Then gently and
sympathetically, he said with sincerity, "I

appreciate how restrictive this temporary confinement is for you, for me, too."

"Claustrophobic. It might feel less of an incarceration had you accepted the many offers of a residence more suitable to a king."

"I disapprove of ostentatious and vulgar displays of power and wealth, too showy for me. I choose not to live any better than the least affluent people I have invited to share this island with me." Malika sighed and rolled her eyes at his naïve idealism, thinking his vows of humble poverty themselves to be pretentious. "The title of king is purely symbolic like a flag, an emblem, or a bumper sticker."

"Yet, you have issued decrees." She reminded him. He remained humble, reverting to his original moniker, Squire Sean. "Not royal decrees as much as advocating tenant rights in my capacity as a glorified landlord. I still wield some influence as the majority property owner."

"At least you could add another bathroom." She teased.

"I can do that if you are going to stay here long enough to make it worth my time."

"I will stay at least until you have trapped your poor unsuspecting best friend into marrying your exotic and mysterious cousin. And what is to keep them from leaving you following the wedding? Have you considered that?"

"Lucia has been traveling the globe since birth. She is done searching, now. She will not again leave home."

"She is an aborigine?" She curiously asked, sounding like a lawyer questioning an evasive witness.

Sean shrugged. "We only recently met each other. I am as much in the dark regarding my newly acquired family, relatively speaking, that is." His words ambling along, aimlessly. "I don't know that she is native to any land; she's a nomadic princess, virtually groundless."

Malika did not pursue this vague response but stared at him momentarily, a curious expression on her face. As Sean stalled by toying with the chess pieces, clearly uncomfortable discussing Princess Lucia in any detail, Malika returned to their previous, unfinished discussion of her "confinement and restricted" movements. She rose from the table and began to pace the room without exchanging more than momentary glances with Sean.

"It might be nice to escape this royal imprisonment occasionally together and reclaim some semblance of a normal social life. If we wish to continue this public charade as passionate lovers, we should look convincingly amorous and affectionate."

"I had no clue that you would agree to that."

"You are still clueless. So, let us play chess." She said with exasperation. Does he not comprehend subtleties at all? She thought to herself.

Although both were longtime and skillful chess players, neither ever really approached

Chess Master status, Sean always insisted on explaining chess strategy to Malika.

"I know how to play chess! If you infrequently win, it is only because I take pity on your surge mentality." She snapped at him.

Nonetheless, he lectured her on board -or in her view -bored, strategy as her chin rested on her tight fist, her eyelids growing heavier with each word, her hand gesturing impatiently, her face expressing annoyance.

"Chess is a game of the intellect, long-term strategies, agonizing patience and psychological warfare, anticipating counterattacks and alternative battlefield maneuvers, always thinking three moves ahead upon battlefields for strategists and tacticians, not for the siege emotionalism for impulsive overreaction."

"Yes, I know." She said crossly. "It's your move."

Chess is how they passed idle time together whenever the conversation faded and repressed their enflamed sexual desires for each other.

Sean, so recently a sober gentleman with an unlimited supply of "Ybani Fruit Juice," was unwilling to risk "making the first move," fearing rejection or offending the young career-minded international lawyer, the "object of his unrequited ardor, affections, and enchantment" since first meeting her.

Malika continually declared on numerous occasions in public and private, for appearances and her professional reputation, her adamant aversion to romantic entanglements. She repeatedly told anyone who asked that she was "definitely" not seeking any long-term commitments, nor did she knowingly send mixed signals to any suitor, to Sean, nor anyone.

She speedily captured his pawns, then his knights and bishops, and then sat back in her chair and smiled triumphantly, waiting for his next futile move.

"Check," She said confidently, "and your queens are in peril."

"Yes," He said, looking directly at her, "I can see that she is."

He groaned desperately, castling his king temporarily out of check then, vainly attempted to throw her off her game with more distracting chatter of protecting your queen resulting in provoking her frowning exasperation.

"A ruthless King may sacrifice a few pawns or all his pawns. He will sacrifice a bishop, surrender a castle or two, even his knights but never ever his queen."

Malika looked up and smiled. "Are you trying to wear down my resistance?"

Sean's face went blank. He shrugged and uttered, "Your move" and sighed as she effortlessly captured his queen.

As Sean studied the board wondering aloud why his king could not send for reinforcements, she pursued the metaphor, "Are you proposing, again?" She asked in a softer, friendlier tone.

"We are just playing chess. I am not proposing a damn thing." He snapped with irritation. Then, toppling his king with a sweep of a backhand, he groaned loudly with disgust, "Fuck it, I give up."

"So easily?" She asked, sympathetically. "If you really desirea direct heir, there are many women eager to marry royalty and some even willing to bear you a child. Not me but someone, somewhere."

"Title chasing superficial, shallow gold-diggers!" He grumbled bitterly.

"You're not a misogynist, are you?" she asked, knowing the answer before asking. Neither Sean nor Alexandre had in her presence and long acquaintance revealed sexist tendencies. Ignorant or naive about women perhaps but never knowingly disrespectful, she thought. Even before his newfound sobriety, she recalled, 'Sean was a happy drunk.'

Sean began arranging the chess pieces for another match when Malika stood, circled the table, and pulled Sean from his chair. "You must be a glutton for punishment, Your Majesty." She walked briskly to the entertainment center, blasting rock music through its speakers, and beckoned Sean to the center of the room. Then, while shoving furniture into the corners of the room, leaving the center of the room empty for dancing, she chastised Sean.

"You are too damn serious! I know you were not always so reserved." She scolded.

Crossing the floor, he smiled, "Only because love drains my energy."

"Come here and dance with me, now!" She laughed.

And he did.

And the crowd of royal watchers could only hear the dance music over the exuberant laughter from inside the king's bungalow. In an instant, the crowd was swept by the music and excitement and began celebrating their king's romance as music unites that which cliques and governments divide.

A Royal Engagement, "You are cordially invited."

Following a lengthy engagement, that the bride thought too long and the groom too sudden, the next decade would open with a royal wedding for Alexandre Begre', the reluctant *heir*, and the ever-reticent Princess Lucia de la Mer.

The wedding ceremony was an unpublicized simple affair, private and secluded on an unidentified, unchartered island with Sean and Malika as Best Man and Maid of Honor as well as signatory witnesses and a non-denominational lay person officiating. Justice Minister Cassandra McGinnis verified the signatures of bride and groom as notary public. When she raised the questions of blood tests and national citizenship and proof of birth, the king waived the formalities. She quietly assented. Only four guests attended the ritual including the parents of the groom, both retired and revered justices having been flown from France along with the wedding party aboard one of the king's royal aircraft. Princess Lucia's regal-looking father King Argus X who naturally *gave the bride away* and her youthful-appearing mother Ysadora VII arrived days earlier to help plan the wedding. When signing the guest book, they simply and illegibly scrawled Greece as their residence.

Interviewed for an unrelated broadcast news segment, the semi-retired general, wealthy arms trader, and defense contractor Eric von Schvinghammer broached the subject of Lucia's lineage by casting the first rippling stone into the conspiratorial waters by demanding that Lucia submit to DNA testing. "Just who the hell is this mysterious princess, what is her nationality and ethnicity?" the general demanded.

The princess shrugged it off with a rehearsed smile and wink. "Are my looks not Aryan enough to please the general?" She laughed. Then, almost as an after-thought, she very softly and casually told the group of reporters, "As any eye can see, I am *Arcadian*. I will not comment on the general's alien conspiracy theory no more." The gushing reporters aside from those from the tabloids, seemed satisfied and pursued the matter no further.

The official reception for Alexandre and Lucia a few months later in the Capitol Pavilion on New Atlantica was a massive, chaotic, and democratic affair. By then, the architects and urban planners were in the final development stages of Capital City having completed the capitol government buildings, streets, avenues, and boulevards, most of the downtown business center, the routes for the solar-powered and all-electric transit system and constructing the family neighborhoods surrounding the urban hub, most of the building supplies and labor provided by future home owners and community volunteers, many of whom had worked previously to build rural homes, farms, ranches and small closely-knit communities. Those outsiders and outcasts rejected by the rural society and cliques were not to be shunned or ostracized but by royal decree retrained and reacclimated to friendlier more accepting neighborhoods and communities.

Large groups of lottery-winning rural dwellers arrived to the wedding reception from across the main island, the small perimeter islets and some from Granito de Ebano by solar powered aerial hover coaches along with the urbanites, debutants, celebrities, socialites, politicos, diplomats, the wealthy elites and philanthropists, patrons of the arts, critics, entertainers, artists and brilliant scientists all mingling together, trading dance partners, engaged in idle conversation or lofty intellectual debate without *incident or conflict, rancor or cliquiness* in the grand ballroom.

Among the uninvited surprise guests hiding in the crowd were the globe-trotting professor Anton Gunter-Ellis accompanied escorting his young wife and former academic intern Amy Logan and the arms dealing general, Eric von Schvinghammer, absent his socially timid, self-conscious wife, the former Mazie Schmidt. The professor dressed modestly not wishing to call attention to himself as a Jake Gillis sponsored *gatecrasher* unlike the general adorned in his full-dress uniform and chest full of self-awarded medals.

Admiral Amanda Danziger and Air Marshal Aung San Maung attended the reception along with numerous other members of the international military family, representing all ranks but without being over-dressed or obtrusive and ever vigilant in their avoidance of the boisterous, braggart General Schvinghammer, having previously set up warning gestures of his approach.

Gillis mingled freely although he too avoided the general and professor, denying that he was aware of their presence despite verification that he had sneaked them back onto the island from their *political wilderness* and furnished them with counterfeit invitations to the gala event.

"How soon may I expect an heir to the throne?" the king demanded of the newlyweds as they tried to sneak away from the ceremony.

"Why don't you produce your own heir?" his cousin, the princess replied.

"That does not appear very promising." Sean scoffed, dejectedly.

"Must we always be your surrogates for everything?" Alexandre added.

"I made You a duke!" Sean countered. "Now, go make me an heir to the throne. This line must continue to keep capitalistic developers from destroying my damn utopia! Finally, the royal couple, the princess and newly anointed duke, managed their escape through a side door as Malika motioned him onto the dance floor. "Why not?" He grumbled in self-pity. "It beats life as a wallflower."

My Kingdom for a Queen.

"I have reconsidered my prior rejections of your offers of marriage. I think you would be wise to marry, if not to find yourself a supportive and affectionate queen, then at least a queen consort for companionship." Malika surprised Sean one evening months later while dining together at an elegant Parisian restaurant.

"Have you someone specific in mind?" He quietly inquired with interest. "Certainly not a title chaser like my late stepmother, the Duchess of Rutherford?"

"Someone strong, courageous, intelligent, utterly patient, wise with a calm, restrained comforting demeanor," she continued, speaking softly, conscious of the overly attentive, eavesdropping diners and waiters, "honest but not overly critical, kind, thoughtful, sophisticated with logical probing analytical mind; socially adept even ascetically pleasing for public affairs yet warm, passionate even seductive during intimacy. As your Queen, she must be elegant, fashionable, and tasteful, of refinement, polished, cultured and poised, formally educated, of impeccable manners in proper ettiq1uette and well versed in International Law and diplomacy."

"I know someone exactly like that who's always refused me."

"Naturally, she would consistently defeat you at chess." She smiled.

"Thank you for your most impressive verbal resume'. I shall take it under advisement." He quickly replied, teasingly.

"I should not wait too long. The offer requires an immediate response." Otherwise, it shall be withdrawn."

"Then, of course, I accept." He grinning, producing a small box containing an engagement ring and blowing off the dust. Then, on bended knee, offering ring he proposed, "Malika Bello, will you please honor and bless me with your hand in marriage?

"How could I possibly refuse?" She smiled, extending her hand.

Sean began to place it on her finger then withdrew while reminding her,

"You have refused on three previous occasions."

"You earned points for resilience. And I did not wish to appear too attainable." She laughed as he slipped the diamond ring upon her finger. They embraced tightly then shared a deep, passionate kiss to the delight of the onlookers.

The Restoration of the Triarchy.

> **"Beware the treacherous return of the Triarchy."**
>
> **—Ybani ambassador.**

The fourth and weakest of the provincial prime ministers, Jasper "Buck" Cannon, a seasoned diplomat but lacking executive training and experience, had surreptitiously summoned Gunter-Ellis and Schvinghammer back to the island kingdom without informing either the king or other ministers, and specifically keeping it guarded secret from Begre' and Cassie McGinnis.

Unofficially, Gunter-Ellis was to serve *behind the scenes* as the de facto foreign affairs adviser and Schvinghammer as island defense adviser, both wielding far more influence than the actual cabinet ministers. No one was to know of their presence on the island as a *deep cover* operation. For two years, they remained underground in luxurious quarters, communicating only with the sputtering, ineffectual prime minister, a bachelor rumored inordinately fond of pubescent boys and girls by showering gifts on them and, of course, the ever-crude, boisterous "self-made" lottery winning billionaire Jake Gillis, an unlikely holdover from the island kingdom's early formation.

It had been hoped that Cannon might clean up the bureaucratic left behind by his immediate predecessor, the inept cocaine-using, black haired, coal-eyed boyish Lord Byron-like "Handsome Hank" Bryce, the youthful gregarious short-term provincial governor, and Bryce's jovial predecessor, the flustered indecisive society matron political wind-swaying Phyllis Morehead, the unknown deputy prime minister thrust into office upon the suspicious, sudden death of the kingdom's first appointed prime minister, the flawlessly honest, straight-laced and bearish but popular and decidedly non-political army field commander Field Marshal Jonathon "Iron Jack" Balfour. Samples of the field marshal's last meal, a favorite of his, a seafood platter and grape juice were analyzed but then the results mysteriously vanished. The cremated body, of course, could not be exhumed and autopsied. Political Dark Horse Balfour might have quickly descended along with Morehead and Bryce into obscurity but for the wealth of endless conspiracy theories surrounding his inexplicable death.

The professor Anton Gunter-Ellis and General Erich von Schvinghammer, the general, even to his wife, family, and his few friends, would not and could not be denied their unquenchable thirst for power, notoriety, and public acclaim; they could not remain buried underground forever, regardless of the plush accommodations. So finally, along with Amy Logan and a small elite cadre, the professor and the general met secretly with Jake Gillis in a dark, dirty, empty warehouse on the eastern outer banks of the main island to plan-or plot -their return to public service.

Conspiracy.

"The worship of the state is the worship of force. There is no more dangerous menace to civilization than a government of incompetent, corrupt, or vile men. The worst evils which mankind ever had to endure were inflicted by bad governments. The state can be and has often been in the course of history the main source of mischief and disaster."

—Ludwig von Mises

Following the tenth anniversary of the monarchy and a series of weak provisional governments, the restless triarchy, Gunter-Ellis and Schvinghammer resenting exile along island-bound Gillis bristling under arbitrary surveillance of his vast entrepreneurial enterprises decided that the time had arrived to replace monarchy and its clumsy, inefficient cabinet-style with an oligarchy (ruled by their triarchy, of course) posing as a republic.

"Why the hell don't we just hold a referendum, election, or something and abolish this goddamn monarchy?" Schvinghammer thundered to Gunther-Ellis and Gillis.

"Because of the charter, General." The professor sighed with an air of impatient superiority. "The monarchy cannot be abolished without the king's assent. He has veto power over legislation and resolutions. There is no sitting legislature, not even the High Court, just Tribunals. The laws are proposed by the king's counselors and his prime minister and cabinet ministers, whom he appointed." The professor sighed. "And we're the ones who suggested a monarchy."

"And I think he likes being king." Gillis attested. "Or playing the part."

The professor coolly continued without emotion. "When Sean Fidwitter, the illegitimate Marquess of Rutherford, took the throne, even he expected it to be temporary until a stable republic could be formed."

"Especially given his vitriolic public criticism of monarchies." Amy Logan said meekly, her voice soft, aware of the general's misogynistic disdain for any female opinion. The general shot a stern glare at her, and she picked up a notepad and pen, justification for her presence at the secret conference.

"Uh, uh, uh!" Gillis stammered in her direction. "We're not taking notes, young lady." The crude billionaire was careful not to behave too abusively. She was no longer an intern running errands and fetching coffee, but the professor's publicly adored wife. "There's to be no damn record of this meeting because it never took place!" Then continuing, he said, "That's why it seemed fuckin' hypocritical when the dumb bastard declared himself king. What a stupid idea, making a drunken nobody a king."

The professor continued, ignoring Gillis' contemptible rudeness. "A recognizable government was essential in forming a country. It is his island. He owned it. He still owns it. He holds exclusive deeds and titles for all perpetuity. He had the option to continue as the benevolent landlord of a restricted private island. We had to convince him that it was unfeasible."

"Yes, the commoner king." The general uttered scornfully.

"And you clowns didn't expect him to fire your incompetent assholes and kick you off his fuckin' island, did you?" Gillis sneered.

"We are not banned or deported. He merely dismissed us from his provisional government." The professor quietly disputed the false conclusion.

"Your services are no longer desired." Amy smiled, mocking the triarchy.

"No longer required!" Her husband, the professor, barked, atypically, at his much younger, attractive, and scholarly wife, his alleged trophy bride.

"That alkie's been playing king for a decade, now," Gillis thundered, without noting Sean's continuous sobriety since their Ybani-hosted business conference, "through what, three, four weak ass provisional governments? That bastard's never going to abdicate, why would he? I sure wouldn't," declared Gillis.

"We know you wouldn't," the general and professor jeered simultaneously.

"As if either of you would surrender power." He contemptuously replied.

Schvinghammer grew impatient. He was intent upon abolishing the monarchy and returning to active duty as general-in-chief of some standing army, ending still another idle retirement. Retirement made him restless, made him feel useless and unwanted, aged him rapidly, and "Damn it!" he was determined never to be old! Like many aging people, he preferred an untimely death to old age.

"We might tacitly support a grassroots movement to abolish the monarchy by planting some charismatic leader, a patsy, so we have plausible denial."

"Sean Fidwitter is an immensely popular king." Amy blurted out, unable to contain herself. "The people love their commoner king! The mob would turn on your treasonous patsy in a minute, they'd mutilate him, defecate and urinate on his corpse, string him up like Mussolini and throw rocks, stones, rotting food, and curse his dead carcass as a traitor!"

"Breathe, my darling girl, breathe." The professor comforted her.

"There are other tactical methods to employ. There is no royal heredity to obstruct us. The Ebonese Queen Consort has not produced an heir." The general grumbled scornfully.

"The king created a royal for her first so there'd be no objection to his marrying a commoner later. I believe he made her the Baroness of Bello?"

"I think barrenness is the operative title here." Gillis laughed, cruelly altering the spelling and meaning of baroness, a pun that went unnoticed.

He repeated several times for effect until Amy pounced on him indignantly.

"Oh, it must be she who's infertile! It couldn't possibly be His Highness, a masculine, virile king, shooting blanks! So, your king could not be sterile?"

"Amy." The professor quietly admonished her as Gillis and the general glared sternly, their misogyny silently deeming it unwelcome and unwanted, demanding she be submissively silent.

"Well, there is an heir apparent, Begre, and the princess has an eight-year-old son, who is next in line to the throne." The professor reminded them.

"That's right, that silly ass king made his lawyer friend Begre' the goddamn Duke of Darwinica, and his other fuckin' lawyer is his Queen

Consort. We're gonna be drownin' in royals if something isn't done soon!"

Gillis roared, alarmingly.

"The boy is no obstacle, merely a low hurdle that can be easily cleared.

The plan will not be compromised, just altered." The general assured them.

Gillis shuffled in his seat, anxiously, then suddenly rose to leave. "Gentlemen, I don't have a horse in this race. I'm out!" He firmly told the others. He was nervous and frightened. "I am not an active participant in this plan. Don't fret. I won't say anything to anyone."

Amy watched from the shadows, smiling at Gillis' atypical anxiety.

"I was never here. I didn't hear this, any of this, not one single word!" Gillis protested as he turned toward the exit.

Schvinghammer's eyes narrowed. He spoke softly, barely above a whisper.

"You've killed before or paid others to kill for you."

"Never a king or president, no political assassinations!" Gillis squirmed.

"There's still blood on your hands, Gillis," shouted the general. "You're a coward, an armchair warrior, a boardroom murderous thief, and complicit!"

Gillis shook his head in excited denial and began to flee from the meeting.

The general motioned, and two hearing impaired sentries blocked the exit. Gillis turned sharply, terrified. He froze. Then the professor calmly approached him, his sleep-inducing, tedious monotone voice non-threatening.

"We are all aware of your 10-year contract with the king, Gillis. It is hardly a well-kept secret bargain. You failed to notice the decade ending, the time clock ticking, and your contract has expired. It will not be renewed."

Gillis retreated, again. "Fine! I don't care! Do your worst. It won't change a damn thing—business as usual. Nothing on me will stick. I'm Teflon!"

"You're not out of it yet, Gillis." The general grinned. "You've heard the name, Cassandra McGinnis?"

Gillis paused at the door, trying to look stone-faced, unconcerned, but his color paled, and his facial muscles twitched. "Yes, the Justice Minister. What about her?"

"We have a mole in her ministry." The professor glanced up, casually.

"A mole?" Gillis's voice trembled slightly.

"Not one of your moles," The professor advised. "Not a mining colony mole."

"A plant. A listening post in our spy network." The general explained. "We have them everywhere, you know. You may have heard that my sons and I have our history with Cassie McGinnis—as well as with Alexandre Begre.

"Cassie McGinnis knows of you and the cartels." The professor interrupted.

"Cartel. What cartel?" Gillis feigned innocently.

"Not cartel. Cartels. Plural cartels." The general emphasized.

"And if the Justice Minister knows," the professor advised them," then her boss, 1st Counselor Begre, also knows or he will as soon as Cassie McGinnis can tell him."

"We know that you're getting a kickback, Gillis," the general said, taking control of the discussion, threatening Gillis with an icy stare and a stern voice, "a large slice of the pie, a seat at the table, a piece of the action. It would behoove you through the cartels to start contributing to my… military readiness campaign and to the professor's what," the general paused, glancing momentarily at Gunter-Ellis before asking," your what, slush fund?"

"Political Action Committee." The professor corrected the general, deceptively. "The king probably does not know about the cartels, but he will be told. Ultimately, your business holdings will be nationalized. You shall all be interminably imprisoned, then deported." He warned Gillis.

"All right," Gillis sputtered angrily. "I'm in, goddammit. I will remind the cartel dons of the terms." The professor, Amy, and the general looked on with interest. "Well," Gillis explained. "In exchange for my guarantee of non-extradition from the island, they are to export their crops and products. They agreed not to market any of their chemical commodities on the island, except for the stimulants used to increase production for the Isla de Granito miners. He scornfully added.

"I can assure that there will be a public outcry by the immigrants. Those people love their king. They'll want justice, and if we fail to convince them of some external conspiracy or give them someone or a group to punish, I predict chaos, a bloodbath, a vicious, vindictive vendetta."

"I can repress anarchy." The general bellowed. "I can decimate any street mob, sissy protesters, rioters, and looters with a real show of force with mass arrests under martial law." The professor winced at the brutal words, especially the word martial law. He had political designs that did not include a military junta. He said nothing for the moment as Amy sidled up to him and squeezed his hand tightly. The general was unabated by disapproving looks. "We're going to need some patsies, low-ranking soldiers, expendables, maybe the Ybanis, those mythical beasts no one's ever seen, the Aquarians!"

"I can sacrifice some of my moles." Gillis offered. "The slackers, injured, weak, and disabled. Let me know how many you need."

"Just enough for public gallows." The general quipped without a smile.

The professor, shocked, gently placed an arm around Amy, comforting her. But she was neither horrified nor repulsed.

"Gentlemen, I believe we should adjourn and reassemble at a time and place to be provided by our friendly host." The professor said.

"Very wise. We have no idea who may be observing or eavesdropping." The general agreed, looking around the room and up at the rafters. "I suggest we depart separately in 15-minute intervals through different doors, employing diverse routes."

Gillis scrambled past the carefully selected hearing-impaired sentries through the main doors, dashing up a blind alley and onto a crowded avenue.

Schvinghammer timed Gillis' departure. Then he left the building through a rear door, calmly marching through a quiet neighborhood to the waterfront, nonchalantly boarding a ferry to the main island, casually chattering with the other passengers.

Awaiting their turn to depart the warehouse, Amy and the professor engaged in idle conversation. To her husband's surprise, Amy suddenly lamented the fates of the king, his queen consort Malika Bello, his best friend, Alexandre Begre, Princess Lucia de la Mer ("of the sea'), and their precocious son. The disposition of Cassie McGinnis remained unclear, her name only arising as the indefatigable justice minister who had discovered the cartels' presence.

"It's too bad." She mused aloud. "I wonder if any of them sought such stature, fame, and power. They are all so beloved, so popular among the masses, celebrated as heroes, like deities."

"When we make gods of our heroes," the professor told her sadly as they departed inconspicuously, "we set them up to fail and ourselves for disappointment."

Chapter Fifteen

COUP D'ÉTAT!

"Most of wars or military coups or invasions are done in the name of democracy against democracy."

—Eduardo Galeano.

"He who intends to kill the guilty sometimes faultlessly sheds the blood of the innocents…"

—Henry Kissinger.

Cassie.

NEW ATLANTICA JUSTICE MINISTER Cassie McGinnis, although not a lawyer herself, was a tireless police investigator who staffed her justice ministry with the best lawyers to guide her dogged pursuit of criminals. She was primarily focused on the often under-prosecuted self-entitled white-collar political, corporate, celebrity, and wealthy elitist culprits who frequently evaded prosecution or received a light reprimand and small fine.

She soon held a press conference, invoking what she prejudicially presumed to be the Spanish language of the cartels, declaring to "root out, dismantle, and disperse from hidden sanctuaries in Greater New Atlantica every vestige of these criminal cartels presently endangering our good and decent, law-abiding citizens and their children as well as the peoples across the globe.

The cartel patróns and capitáns, dons and capos, asesinos and soldares shall find no quarter here to engage in their illegal drug and human trafficking operations. They shall know the full weight and harshest penalties permitted under the law: fines, incarceration, extradition, and permanent deportation.

It was an unusual and combative tone for the soft-spoken and composed former army captain, leading many to wonder if the false accusations during her military trial years before had seriously affected her entire persona and temperament.

"All right, that's it, Gillis!" Shouted the Chief Don, Philip Anderson, of the cartels. "You guaranteed us complete immunity, sanctuary with no extradition!"

"Yes, that was when my sales commission was 30 percent."

"You prick! Are you shaking us down? Us? Do you know who we are, what we've done in the past, what we'll do to you?" The Don threatened. "You could vanish into thin air like Earhart, Hoffa, and the dinosaurs!"

The bulky drug lord and procurer did not intimidate Gillis. He squeezed the don and the menacing enforcers, smugly with a confident smile.

"It's bold talk and hyperbole." Gillis calmly told them.

"Hyperbole?" The Don stared blankly. He turned toward his bewildered bodyguards, who shrugged. Then, puzzled by Gillis' fearlessness, they all stared at him with renewed respect and listened in awe.

"It's all political posturing for the public." He said, unfamiliar with Cassie's courageous zeal and unflinching determination.

"Before she can raid your processing plants, she'll need a warrant signed by a judge." Amy reminded them.

"Where she's gonna to find a judge? There ain't hardly no goddamn judges, there ain't even no traffic courts!" Gillis blurted out.

"Because there's no traffic but foot traffic," Amy interjected.

"Begre' and the prime minister, Cannon, are still developing the judicial system. Cannon is delaying the process for us, insisting on top-down appointments to the High Court first." The professor patiently explained.

"That's just stupid!" The Don grumbled.

"You're complaining about no courts?" Amy sneered with brave sarcasm.

The Don glared at her. "Who are you? Why are you here?" He yelled.

"This young, intelligent lady is my wife." The professor answered firmly.

"We didn't bring our wives!" The general objected. "Wives don't belong here!"

"Do you ever…take her anywhere, General?" Amy confronted him. Then turning steely-eyed to the Don and Gillis. "Do you honor and respect women? Do you even have wives or just prostitutes?" She demanded defensively, aware of the disparaging gossip that she was merely a young, airheaded trophy wife.

"All right! Now you can just shut the fuck up!" Gillis shouted at her.

The professor stepped between them, protecting Amy, raising his hands to de-escalate the anger. "Gentlemen, we have an agenda to follow." He looked directly at the Don. "The king must sign off on all deportations. Once we all agree upon the method, the issue can be resolved. We must all be protected by plausible deniability; we cannot permit any of it to be traced back to any of us, to this room. Therefore, we cannot personally hire assassins nor risk even the appearance of a military coup. The provincial militias are all fiercely loyal."

"Patsies. We need pasties! Disguised as some expendable fringe group, malcontented slackers or race we want to eliminate, anyway!"

"I guess that means my Dispensables." The Don nodded.

"How soon will they be ready?" the professor asked.

"The moment I give the word."

"This meeting is adjourned." The professor announced, and once more as before, they all filed out of the warehouse, separately through different exits at 10-minute intervals.

Pete.

The exotic, arcane Princess Lucia de la Mer conceived almost immediately, waiting to consummate her torrid romance with Alexandre Begre' until the wedding night. Throughout their courtship and subsequent engagement, she had kept her suddenly amorous fiancé at bay, resisting his many seductive advances like a traditional Victorian-age bride. When her pregnancy became most physically evident within five weeks, even her obstetrician remarked on how early she was showing.

"We have concerns about your curious lab results, Your Highness. We want to rerun them."

"There will be no need for that." The princess said crisply, ending the transmission.

As she approached the eighth week of her pregnancy, her stomach enlarged to make her appear 14-16 weeks pregnant. The princess had employed a doula who helped her and accompanied her by rejoining her parents at some distant, undisclosed location. Alexandre pleaded that she remain at home with him, promising her the most comfortable surroundings and the best medical care and personal staff available.

It was to no avail. She insisted she would bear their firstborn in more comfortable familial settings of her childhood and adolescence. "I do not wish you distracted from your neglected legal profession nor your obligations to the king any more than our courtship and marriage have already done." She said sweetly, her radiance spellbinding him.

Then, promising to telecast him weekly on her health and condition, she told him, "He shall bring you home your son, a handsome and healthy crown prince."

"How can you possibly know it will be a boy without an ultrasound?"

"Because my husband, it is my destiny to perform this one task."

Then, she took his face in her soft hands, her long, delicate, outstretched fingers on his cheeks, and kissed his lips passionately.

When he awoke the next morning, the princess and her doula had departed not to return with their infant son for one year. Only her doula, parents, family, obstetrician, and medical staff could know but never reveal that her gestation period was six months. Still, she remained gone and out of the public eye for a whole year for the sake of appearances.

Alexandre and Lucia had chosen to name their son, Pete, simply without explanation. "I explain nothing." The enigmatic princess remained unexplained to intrusive journalists and throngs of royalty watchers and celebrity worshippers, living vicariously through the obscene wealth and unearned fame of shallow narcissists. Strangers meeting the child for the first time insisted that Pete must be a nickname, for proper names Peter, paternally Pierre, or due to an unascertained maternal lineage, guessed Pietro or Petros. It was the precocious boy himself who most frequently corrected them, telling sternly, "No. My name is Pete. Pete Begre'." Then he would walk away with one or both parents wishing to hear no more of this nonsense.

Sunset on the Monarchy.

Throughout his halcyon days in New Atlantica, first as the altruistic benefactor and benevolent squire, then as the commoner king, Sean enjoyed unilateral popularity among the grateful people in the provinces, the provincial militias fiercely loyal to him, the affection of Ybanis, and the apparent dormancy of the island's First Beings, the Aquarians. This period of utopian serenity had blinded him to any risk and personal danger. It simply is inconceivable that any individual, group, or faction would or could wish him harm. Whenever anyone near him, his trusted friend Alexandre, his "cousin" Princess Lucia, or Queen Consort Malika, whom he continued to adore, even worship, loving her more deeply each day as time passed, warned him of dangerously subversive elements anywhere within his kingdom, he politely and quickly discounted the idea.

Despite his dismissals, dark storm clouds were indeed hovering above Sean Fidwitter's island kingdom, and the sunlight was fading.

Plausible Deniability.

"None of this can be traced back to us. We must all have plausible deniability." The professor continually warned Schvinghammer and Gillis, who had both grown weary of hearing it.

The general then firmly declared, "We need to keep Old Buck Cannon out of the loop. He's too indecisive and pliable, trying to please all factions, liberals, conservatives, moderates, and extremists at once. I don't trust him not to sway with the next wind change."

"That sounds more like Handsome Hank Bryce to me, usually too stoned to govern." Grumbled Gillis. "And they're both better than Phyllis Morehead."

"Because they're men, right?" Amy replied with bitter sarcasm.

"In all fairness, Cannon was a fairly competent diplomat back in his day." The professor defended the nerve-racked prime minister. "He's exhausted from old age and Begre's constant interference."

"Well, I like the old boy myself." Gillis asserted. "I've always found him to be very reasonable."

Amy again snipped at Gillis. "Uh huh, corruptible, bribable, rapacious."

"Your words, Missy." He snapped back with contempt. "I said, reasonable."

"All right, you two. Enough!" The professor lectured them.

Then Schvinghammer stepped between the sparring pair and the professor, directing his concerns to the professor, the self-appointed, titular leader of the group. "What about that Don, what's his damn name? Do we take him into our clique?"

"Anderson, Philip Anderson." Amy spoke, then murmuring to herself, with surprise, "That's innocuous enough for a crime boss. Do you men wish to be affiliated with a cold-blooded, vicious killer?" She exclaimed with astonishment.

"I don't know that he's ever personally murdered anyone." Gillis demurred.

"All right, but he's had people killed. His hands are stained with innocent blood!" She argued.

Gillis shrugged. "Well, I don't know how innocent they were."

"It doesn't matter. We cannot permit ourselves to be linked to him or his organization." The professor calmly told them. "If he uses his people for this task, fine! But we are in no way connected to it, officially or unofficially. Our hands are to remain clean, our names unsullied."

"Then precisely what is our role?" The general demanded.

"Have you never stove cooked anything, General? Have you never stirred the pot?" the professor smiled deviously.

Disposable Contract.

Don Felipe (Philip Anderson) was growing impatient with the triarchy. His spies had reported that Justice Minister Cassie McGinnis and First Counselor Alexandre Begre' were exerting intense pressure on the king to prepare to move swiftly against the cartels once their teams had gathered enough evidence for a prima facie criminal case.

Jake Gillis, he told the other Dons during a meeting in his palatial home, was over-confident about his decade-long hands-off agreement with the king. "Pass the word to the capos and capitáns." He ordered. "The patróns unanimously approved the resolution."

The entire Executive Commission nodded in unilateral agreement, one of the Dons exclaiming. "Activate the asesinos and soldares!"

"No, Don Barkley, we're using dispensables as patsies," Felipe explained.

"The dumb fucks are gonna think it's their membership initiation." Added the consigliere.

The Dons and Capos burst into cruel, hysterical laughter, then adjourned to the liquor cabinet.

An Audience with the King.

"What the herd hates the most is the one who thinks differently. It is not so much the opinion itself, as the audacity of wanting to think for themselves. Something they do not know how to do."

—Arthur Schopenhauer.

"If there is anything the nonconformist hates worse than a conformist, it's another nonconformist who doesn't conform to the prevailing standard of nonconformity."

—Bill Vaughn.

Having been constantly and unmercifully goaded by the Triarchy and Don Philip Anderson and his Executive Commission, the titular head of government the prime minister Jasper Cannon continuously appealed through electronic communications to "His Majesty" proposing a Constitutional Convention, naturally chaired by Gunter-Ellis, to establish a presidential republic, the executive power being shared by a popularly elected president and parliamentary-appointed head of government, prime minister.

The king repeatedly ignored the communiques, deleting each one and shredding the hard copies (paper) into the proverbial File #13, the shredded recycle bin. "What a waste of paper resources." He scoffed. "Doesn't that fool know I'm a planet preservationist?"

Eventually to bring an end the annoying badgering, the king granted an audience to his prime minister and the triarchy with the understanding that his trusted legal advisors, First Counselor Begre' and Queen Consort Malika would be present at the meeting. Don Felipe, however, was not to be included, being under investigation for probable criminal indictment.

With his queen and best friend at his side, the king listening patiently even when Prime Minister Cannon following several moments of transparent fawning bloviation, "Your kind altruism has secured your place in the annals of world history as a kind and compassionate monarch, as our charitable benefactor and a living symbol of active egalitarianism. We thank you, Your Majesty, for your unselfish service." Then he modestly and awkwardly stepped aside in deference to the king's old nemesis Professor Anton Gunter-Ellis who argued for bureaucratic Meritology at agonizing length eventually arriving to the point, that the king should graciously abdicate once a presidential republic could be established with a president, prime minister a unicameral parliament and a federal court system. I beg Your Majesty's indulgence and endorsement for the creation of a new republic by his generous abdication and the preservation of his beloved destiny. We shall with your approval, provide you with a permanent residence, comfortable pension, and adequate expense account."

As Queen Consort Malika nudged King Sean I to awaken him, the professor bowed politely and surrendered the lectern to General Erich von Schvingheimer.

The general monotonous presentation was too familiar and entirely predictable. Sean, Malika and Alexandre tried to stay alert and listen politely but soon were nodding out of sheer boredom as the general repeated the same old grind, demanding a standing army supported by national taxes, lottery, or user fees. As usual he wanted overall command of the standing army and militias and an immediate field promotion to Field Marshal. Snapping to attention, he clicked his heels together and saluted, uttered the words. "God bless Your Majesty and Long Live the New republic." Then he sharply stepped away from the lectern.

When Jake Gillis took the lectern, both Queen Consort Malika and the professor's young "trophy wife," Amy Logan sat up, glaring contemptuously at the corrupt corporate raider, their contempt obvious.

Queen Malika found Gillis nauseating and repulsive for his crudeness and criminality. She found his demeanor and bad manners so disgusting that she abhorred being in the same room, even a large ballroom, with him. Her suspicions that Gillis held some secret over the king's head enraged her, leading to several arguments and her repeated refusals to marry him. Her persistent demands that her husband confide in her the details of his "special business arrangement" with Gillis long before their betrothal often infuriated her. Sean would not reveal anything, declined to even discuss the matter, and frustrated her further when he quietly turned and walked away. As quarreling escalated with Malika's voce rising to a shouting, to a screaming pitch, Sean grew steadily quieter until he silently departed, returning hours later having given her ample time to compose herself. Then her calm attempts to reopen the topic, even seductively, were in vain.

Amy Logan eycd Gillis with undisguised hatred and unrestrained contempt for all to see. The professor's public association with Gillis, she believed, was harmful to the political aspirations that he had harbored since his youth. **"You are judged by the company you keep."** She frequently paraphrased **Aesop** to her erudite husband's condescending annoyance. "It's only a casual acquaintance." he told her, "For political expediency."

As Gillis began his presentation—his tedious old familiar refrain—Malika curtly and rudely cut him off before he started on a free market devoid of cumbersome regulation, government interference, labor unions and adequate wage demands.

"What the fuck are you doing here, you goddamn swindler, you crook, you fucking criminal?" Malika shouted curtly, abandoning all regal composure. Alexandre smiled, covering his mouth to control his laughter. Sean shifted his weight in his cushioned chair nervously, his face blushing with embarrassment. "How is it you are not in prison doing hard time?" She demanded.

" Because goddammit, I ain't done a goddamn fuckin' thing illegal." Gillis shouted, forgetting his place in the presence of Queen Consort. The king rose from his chair, glaring steely eyed at Gillis, "I ain't committed no crime, I ain't been charged with a goddamn fuckin' thing!"

"You haven't been indicted… as of **yet.**" Alexandre said quietly and confidently.

Gillis's tantrum exploded. Between a litany of profanity, he incoherently demanded an end to the monarchy, cursing the existence of monarchies in the Second Millennium, shouting, **"Revolt godfuckindammit revolt!"**

The sentries surrounded him quickly, twisting his arms behind him and shoving him unceremoniously out of the room as he struggled to break free of their grip, kicking screaming more obscenities at the monarchs.

The professor knelt apologetically and humbly before the king and queen. "This is not why we are here, Your Majesties," He said, apologetically, then nodding toward Begre', he added, "Your Grace." Acknowledging Begre's non-hereditary dukedom. "We implore your Majesties' forgiveness for any disrespect uttered in the heat of anger to Her Most Royal Majesty, the Queen." He spoke humbly, tactfully omitting "Consort" in his delicate retreat.

After Gillis had been unceremoniously ejected by the sentries, Gunter-Ellis and Schvinghammer politely bowed to both monarchs with a nod to the duke, awaiting either admonishment or approval of their presentation from the king.

"I shall take this under advisement." Sean told them, evasively as he regally dismissed them with a slight wave of the hand. Malika smiled at him proudly, tenderly placing her hand onto his.

Then, obeying royal protocol, the professor and general backed respectfully and deferentially out of the room.

Amy Logan lingered for a moment, bowing then curtsying to the royal couple, explaining, "I am but a meek commoner without agenda, Your Majesties." She spoke with transparent, unconvincing servile flattery. "I simply wanted to meet the king and queen."

They nodded toward her pleasantly. She curtsied once more, quietly wished them long, prosperous, and serene lives, and backed out of the room.

Complicity.

"**The world is governed by very different personages from what is imagined by those who are not behind the scenes.**"

—Benjamin Disraeli.

"**Everyone wants power; let them have it. Your goal is not power. Your goal is the illusion of surrendering power.**"

—Neil Peter Christy,
Head Lion.

Amy Logan made it explicitly clear that she wanted the king and especially Alexandre Begre out of her husband's path to power, fame, and glory. New Atlantica is just a stepping-stone to even greater heights of power and world acclaim. "The king is a foolish and silly, empty-headed puppet." She was now pulling the professor's strings. "That troublemaking lawyer Begre' is the real danger." She frequently whispered to him as they lay in bed together. "He has the king's ear." As she seductively had his. "He's the puppeteer and the royal ventriloquist." She reminded him. "You'll never be president as long as your damn honor student (Begre') stands in your way. He has his ambitions if not for himself then for his son, the crown prince, can you believe the name, Pete Begre'?"

The professor, once a strong and decisive political manipulator in his own right, was compliantly under his wife's thumb, much to his co-conspirators' and the general public's delight and amusement, doing her bidding.

The general Erich von Schvinghammer was far less cunning and much more conspicuous. He coveted a junta under his command following a military coup. But he was prevented from acting always under the ever-watchful, suspicious eyes of the Alliance of Nations and the rivalry of the other conspiracy plotters.

Gillis, for his part, had lost control of the cartels. Don Philip Anderson was the *wild card*, refused to be constrained. He was eager to move against the monarchy by empowering his *dispensables* to act. Secretly, Gillis desired the cartels' failure. He briefly flirted with exposing them to the king's guard, the royal police force, the militias, and the Justice Ministry, but fears for his safety, for his very life terrified him so he kept his silence and remained complicit.

FLIES on Walls.

> "To treat another human being as if they're expendable is the very definition of evil."
>
> —Marty Rubin.

The flies—as the spies were called to differentiate them from the moles, as the rock miners on Isla de Granito de Ebano were known- were virtually everywhere! With no spy-free zones, they migrated beyond past physical boundaries, fences, across terrains and oceans. There was virtually no place, civilized or uncivilized that they wouldn't go-to intermingle and merge among diverse groups without arousing a casual disinterested glance let alone suspicion. They tended to gather in shadows, inconspicuous out of sight but still within listening range, no longer in the underground. They now lived in abundance atop the soil in steadily growing numbers, freely roaming the landscapes of international governments, the private secluded offices of high finance, wealthy corporations, the trade unions, among the workers at their jobs, with the sharpest hearing. Their voices never raised, loud, boisterous, or shrill. These spies are extremely quiet and frequently silent, speaking in a whisper. They represented the perfect guest. But they were never harmless.

The Dispensables: MOB HIT.

Eighteen brave young Dispensable soldiers, still young enough to believe in their invincibility, received their instructions and pay from the Dons, then departed, slithering across the landscape under the cover of darkness, dressed as guerrillas to the main island's northernmost tip overlooking the Darwin Straits. As they crept under the jungle canopy as quietly and softly as sure-footed felines, careful not to alert any creatures or humans by clumsily snapping twigs underfoot in the underbrush, stooping under branches rather than to alarm anything or anyone by brushing against them, none of the more seasoned cadre could escape the feeling that they were being silently observed by some entity with every step though the none of the scouts, the flanks (left and right sides) the point (lead scout)nor 'sixes" (rear) observed Any movement, creatures, animals or beings, heard any strange noises but their own breathing and racing hearts nor smelled any scents or aromas but the team members' sweety body odors.

Using night vision binoculars and GPS, the scouting party paused on a small knoll as the early dawn light filtered through the fog. Then, silently dispersing on their hands and knees in different directions, viewed the king's residence from all four angles. With alarm, they stared at the compound in disbelief. As quietly as possible, the communication specialist texted a frantic warning to the platoon officer and top sergeant of imminent danger.

The Ybanis, too, had inconspicuous, invisible spies conducting espionage by ingratiating themselves among every camp, group, and organization throughout the main island. But they reported not to the king due to his fatalistic complacency to danger and threats on his life, but directly to Justice Minister Cassie McGinnis, First Counselor Alexandre Begre, and to the Queen Consort Malika Bello through inaudible, undetectable telepathy.

Upon joining the scouts on the *dew*-soaked knoll under a reddish early morning sun, the rest of the "hit squad" immediately observed the dilemma.

A thick perimeter of Ybani combat-ready warriors stood shoulder-to-shoulder, a dozen rows thick, towering above the front flanks of militia home guard and groups of zealous volunteers who poured out of pubs, taverns, and saloons, grabbed hunting gear, rifles, shotguns, and ammunition from home to back up militias from all the provinces. Their combined stoic unflinching *loyalty* to their altruistic benefactor was written in their hearts and ingrained in their stern faces, ready to die in battle to protect Sean I (formerly Fidwitter), their beloved commoner king.

The captain immediately aborted the mission regardless of the dire consequences for disobeying the Dons.

"A suicidal assault without survivors!" The top sergeant concurred.

"We'll all be slaughtered, massacred!" Another sergeant exclaimed.

The soldiers declared, "Full membership isn't worth this shit!"

"Fuck this! I'm going home, goddammit!" Shouted a recruit.

The captain nodded, "Withdraw."

"Withdraw? Screw that! Retreat!" A sergeant yelled.

With the captain and the top sergeant bringing up the rear, the Hit Squad turned and fled through morning fog, some tossing their weapons and black guerrilla attire aside as they sprinted in chaotic terror.

The captain had failed to assign guards to protect the rear flank. He soon arrived to find the entire contingent team of untrained, confused would-be assassins captured and under guard. The captain sighed, and the top sergeant cursed but raised their arms to submissively surrender.

Not a single shot had been fired, the only casualties being wounded pride and diminished egos.

Disposing of the Dispensables.

None of the Hit Squad, especially its leaders, the captain and sergeants, were eager—even willing—to report the failed mission to the dons and capos. Whispering nervously among themselves, they believed based on reputation that the Ybanis and immigrant militia and volunteers would not be subjected to the torture expected from the angry, brutal mob bosses. Some even believed their lives would be spared to be imprisoned in comfortable housing, provided with nutritious food, fresh drinkable water, and minimal discipline.

One prisoner even suggested the prison time would be short and that they might all be pardoned or released from captivity.

"Oh great," chided a cynical prisoner, "Pardon us back to the bosses, a fate worse than death!"

"It would be death," chided another, "slow and painful!"

They were released within days through the intervention of the compassionate king, having been encouraged by Begre.' Cassie urged harsher terms, life sentences in some small, distant jungle island prison with rats and snakes for cellmates in shark-infested waters. The king stipulated that none were to be repatriated to their former employers but safely escorted to the outer banks and perimeter islands, then transported back to their native lands with new identities, clothes, and a stipend to discourage recidivism while they secured honest employment. The Queen Consort, however, insisted on one more stipulation, fearing for her husband's safety against retaliation and revenge, that they all be permanently exiled from Greater New Atlantica and never be allowed to return.

"Why would they be pissed at me? I just sent them home with new clothes and spending money," the king laughed.

"You're too good for this world." She answered and followed with a loving embrace and kiss.

"Now what do we do about the dons and capos?" Begre' wanted to know.

"We prosecute the sons-of-bitches!" Cassie answered with fervor.

An Alternative Plan.

"The mob creates nothing; it can only destroy."

—Herbert Hoover.

The aging and nerve-wrecked prime minister (P.M.) Buck Cannon died suddenly of a cerebral hemorrhage, a mere seven weeks following the aborted mob hit, replaced by his deputy, p.m., Breck Ridgeway. Ridgeway, the youngest P.M. to date at 36, had political ambitions of his own, to become the republic's first and powerful president the minute the monarchy was abolished. Ridgeway was impatient. His plan involved arresting the king on spurious capital charges and having the king and his entire court publicly executed.

Gunter-Ellis, in a hastily scheduled meeting with the new P.M., reminded him of the King's Charter, making the sovereign inviolable, that all legislation, statutory motions, and legal acts required the sovereign's approval, signature, and official seal.

"The king," the professor explained, "is protected by strict Sovereign Immunity. The sovereign is not legally liable for civil or criminal offenses. Even if prima facie evidence was presented in a court of law, he remains immune from prosecution."

Ridgeway listened politely but remained unconvinced. He was neither impressed nor pliable as were his predecessors. He hungered for the power of the presidency and to use that power freely and fully once he obtained it.

Alarmed that he was about to be cast aside into the political wilderness once again, this time by a power-seeking political newcomer instead of the king and his royal court, the professor alerted the general and Jake Gillis.

With Amy wide-eyed, silently watching, Gunter-Ellis informed his associates about the new, ambitious P.M., sharing his concerns.

"Well, we put that uncooperative shit on the throne in the first place. I don't see any damn reason why we can't remove the bastard!" The general railed.

"I know the Dons are planning another hit. Why not let them take care of it? That would leave all of us completely in the clear." Gillis offered.

"Gentlemen, our immediate problem is not the king but Ridgeway. He's a greater threat to our plans than is the sovereign." Gunter-Ellis reminded them.

"Then, why not take them both out at the same time?" Gillis asked as a thought more than a question. "And Begre' too! We have someone to do the hit and take the fall for it."

"I'm still in favor of a military operation." The general grumbled.

"We know you are, General, a junta." The professor sighed, rolling his eyes in a sarcastic tone.

"I may have a thought." Amy finally interrupted quietly. "Take out the prime minister and the full cabinet except the Justice Minister McGinnis and lay the entire murderous plot at the doorstep of the king, like a *reverse coup,* a desperate act to preserve the monarchy. But, not right away," she added, "first you must stir up the masses. Otherwise, they will remain loyal to their…" She paused before concluding with caustic, bitter sarcasm, "beloved king."

Class Warfare: Inciting the Masses.

"Where justice is denied, where poverty is enforced, where ignorance prevails, and where any one class is made to feel that society is an organized conspiracy to oppress, rob and degrade them, neither persons nor property will be safe."

—Frederick Douglass.

"Every man who repeats the dogma of Mill that one country is no fit to rule another country must admit that one class is not fit to rule another class."

—Bhimrao Ramji Ambedkar.

The next three years were spent by the triarchy which now embraced the inclusion of the scheming Amy Logan, fanning out across the provinces in a well-orchestrated but subtle plan to incite the masses against the institution of the monarchy if not directly against the immensely popular king himself then those influential powers behind the throne, the Queen Consort Malika Bello, First Counselor Alexandre Begre' and Justice Minister Cassie McGinnis.

Gunter-Ellis, much to Gillis' disapproval, portrayed himself as the Socialist friend of Labor, lecturing on "the emerging income disparities between the privileged employers and employees," and emphasizing the gaudy, unearned, nearly obscene, ostentatious luxurious lifestyles of the wealthy created at the expense, sweat, toil and immoral exploitation of the underpaid, unappreciated working class."

In closed quarters, Gillis objected to the professor's "class war baiting," telling the professor, "all this stirring up the masses shit is just going to come back on us!"

When the professor demurred, Gillis protested that the formerly homeless and destitute immigrants "have never had it so fuckin' good."

"We know that, but they don't." Replied the professor. "I am taking advantage of their ignorance. I think I can persuade them that they were brought here under pretenses to benefit the "undeserving lazy upper classes."

Some of the unrest in the provinces began peacefully. At the same time, other incidents were violent, without any outside agitation over property intrusions and trespassing, border conflicts, military conscription, relocation orders, and escalated neighborhood disagreements. Provincial militias staged "sit-down strikes" refusing mobilization into Schvinghammer's National Standing Army. As the recently appointed Defense Minister, the general threatened mass arrests and worse, an order to fire on the defiant militia by his mercenaries (secretly funded by Gillis and the Cartels). The governors contacted First Counselor Alexandre Begre through the Justice

Minister. Begre immediately intervened and personally confronted the general, citing the King's Charter that there was to be "no standing army" or any foreign military installations anywhere on the archipelago. The general blustered angrily, claiming full command of the militia and the right to conscription as Defense Minister.

"You serve at the pleasure of His Majesty; the king and I speak with full authority as his legal counsel. "Stand down, General, or you are dismissed from the King's Cabinet forthwith!" The general withdrew, muttering threats and profanities under his breath.

> **"A woman needs a man like a fish needs a bicycle."**
>
> **—Gloria Steinem.**

Meanwhile, Amy Logan was hosting soirees with the women in the provinces ostensibly to promote book clubs, fashion, "girl talk," and idle conversation of "concern to women" rather than to foment radical feminism and marital rebellion. Her approach was always subtle, never controversial or confrontational. She and the women politely but firmly refused the requests from husbands as well as single men seeking to attend the soirees to leer at the professor's beautiful young trophy wife. And soon, wives and mothers were rebelling against all the traditional, subservient gender roles, assuming managerial roles in the household, restructuring the hierarchy, and reassigning the menial household tasks to husbands and children. "What if we refuse to do it?" The family members defiantly protested. "Then it won't get done." The women shrugged complacently as they darted out the door to Amy's next seminar on the "Roles of Independent Womanhood."

As the complaints and rumors, primarily from the husbands and sons, began to filter back to the royal court, the king shrugged without comment. He deferred silently to Queen Consort Malika Bello, who had continued using her last name. "Malika Fidwitter, seriously?" she had uttered at the wedding altar. "The king and I do not see this as a bad thing." She told the complaining males. "In the matter, we are amused." She smiled, mocking the Victorian Age.

"If women truly wish equality with men, they're going to have to surrender an awful lot of power and influence." The professor grumbled quietly to himself.

> **"An imbalance between rich and poor is the oldest and most fatal ailment of all Republics."**
>
> **—Plutarch.**

Gillis, through his surrogates, continued to stir up the masses against the monarchy while employing cartel thugs to break heads, strikes, and quash labor movements. Labor organizers, ringleaders, and agitators began to vanish in the night until the labor force became fearful to even grumble among themselves about stagnate or reduced wages, long work hours, unsafe factory conditions, and declining benefits. Gillis planted agitators, however, encouraged anti-monarchy sentiments, focusing on the disparity between the privileged entitlement of the royalty at the expense and exclusion of the working poor.

In truth, no such disparity existed. The king and his court lived modestly: "I should never be better off than those who toil and sweat for a living." The egalitarianist king repeated frequently.

Judicial Appointments.

During the eleventh year of the monarchy, the triarchy and cartels were unexpectedly disrupted when the king appointed Bertram Dawson as the Chief Administrative Judge of the new National Tribunal. This tribunal was the highest court in the country, overseeing the legality, fairness of trials, verdicts, punishments, and ensuring ethical standards in lower court decisions. "Old Bert" was not appointed as a jurist but in his familiar role as an administrator, managing the docket for the Tribunal. His task was to establish a nationwide judicial system by facilitating a non-partisan council of jurists, attorneys, and legal scholars to recommend jurist appointments across all courts by the king and his non-political privy council.

Suddenly, without fanfare, a judicial system was formally established to legally adjudicate both criminal and civil litigations on the island, ranging from minor offenses to capital cases. Cassie McGinnis' legal team was already preparing legal briefs to prosecute Gillis and the cartels. The Schvinghammer family, which had once falsely accused her of atrocities during the early explorations of New Atlantica, also feared prosecution should Cassie vindictively desire vengeance.

Jake Gillis Warns the Cartels.

Jake Gillis whispered into the ear of Don Felipe (Philip Anderson) to alert his dons and capos that Cassie McGinnis and the eager new politically ambitious P.M., Breck Ridgeway, finally had a system of courts where they could indict and prosecute the cartels—or anyone else they pleased.

"It might be wise to act on your plans before the judges begin issuing search and arrest warrants or orders of deportation. But, of course, that's up to your discretion. My hands are tied." Gillis' hands, of course, were not tied. He desired to invoke with some credibility the clean hands rule, should his past involvement with criminal elements and the cartels result in his being indicted as a co-defendant or subpoenaed as a material witness testifying against his former associates in the cartels.

To maintain a safe distance from the criminal elements, Gillis busied himself with his sundry industrial, business, and philanthropic land acquisitions ostensibly for public welfare and to improve working conditions. Keeping a watchful eye and an ear to the ground, Gillis' private security police warned immediately of the alarming presence of environmental activists and labor union agitators. Posters were hung on factory walls, handbills distributed along with scurrilous word-of-mouth campaigns warning wage earners of the many crucial jobs lost or deemed obsolete overnight due to strict environmental over-regulation and closed shops and worker intimidation by racketeering and corrupt, pension-stealing labor organizers. Rank and file workers were advised to ignore union agitators outside the gates, never to speak or even nod to them, and to refuse their communist-inspired literature. Security guards made notes of persons engaging with the petitioners, collected their employee identification badges, and denied entry into the workplace. The unrestricted use of fists, clubs, and brutal beatings of defiant laborers sent a loud and clear warning to the labor force. "Anyone who doesn't like it here is free to quit anytime. But good luck finding another job anywhere on the island." The message was clear. The Cartels and Gillis Enterprises represented island monopolies.

Schvinghammer, the Militias and the Border Wars.

The general's mercenaries, volunteers, and loyal soldiers infiltrated the militia ranks incognito to cleverly provoke dissension in the ranks, by using subliminal messages and subversion tactics to lower morale suggestive of an aristocratic hierarchy and unfair class system. The infiltrators first subtly and surreptitiously indoctrinated the lowest-ranking soldiers with suggestive morale-lowering tactics and psychological warfare, subjected to petty harassment as lowly untouchable serfs, constantly harassed, belittled, degraded, and mistreated, not unlike inciting starving Russian peasants preceding the 1917 Leninist Bolshevik revolution or the impoverished farmers and peasants following Mao in the Chinese Revolution of 1949. The privates soon resented anyone wearing stripes, especially NCOs, whom they bitterly and unfairly stereotyped as inept, clipboard-carrying lifers (who can't make it on the outside, and both were encouraged by the officers as elitist snobbish swells. Having infiltrated and disrupted the morale and esprit de corps, rendering the provinces' militia and home guard ineffective for border disputes, territorial acquisitions, and urban annexations, he recruited his two eldest sons, Wilhelm, and Ernst along with their undercover intelligence staff to pose as new immigrants claiming squatter rights on lands already granted to the original settlers. Other agents slipped surreptitiously among the original settlers to instigate arguments over grazing and water rights and property lines using counterfeit deeds. As conflicts heated up among all the immigrants, the Schvinghammer brothers stepped back to watch in amusement. Still, they faded into the shadows to avoid the fates of their younger brothers, Hans and Karl, especially with Alexandre Begre' and Cassie McGinnis lurking about the island.

General Schvinghammer, making himself available but not too obvious, gracefully acquiesced to the Provincial governors' appeal to reorganize the militias into one cohesive (illegal) standing army, introduced national conscription, rigid training, restore order by reducing dissension, disciplining insubordinate soldiers and go on to claim full credit for successfully and peacefully concluding the Colonial Wars, as the border conflicts and the property disputes were called.

Gunter-Ellis, A Democratic Republic.

The professor was charged with the most delicate and challenging mission to subtly convince the immigrants, the masses, and citizens, formerly homeless and indigent, to abolish the monarchy and establish an elective republic. These were the appreciative recipients of generous, tax-free land grants, housing assistance, free public education, vocational training, and employment placement, all provided at no cost by Sean the Benefactor and the beloved Commoner King. The most vital services, police, fire, and healthcare, were available to all funded payroll deductions, industrial and commercial contributions from public land, and liberal zoning user fees. Due to the nearly 100% active participation, the publicly invested revenues always exceeded the expenditures, as most of the public rarely required the services due to a high rate of active volunteerism and healthy lifestyles.

Other public services were available but not required through a "cafeteria plan" where employees made individual contributions that their employers matched by mandate.

The poor working conditions at Gillis Enterprises were a well-guarded secret and unreported by frightened workers. In any case, those workers were likely to rebel and riot against the Jake Gillis Management Team than to attribute any blame to the king. The king, living modestly on (still an anonymous donor) a trust fund since the untimely death of his mother, had declined tax revenues to support his monarchy.

"This is not the goddamn Middle Ages, and I am a far cry from Richard the fuckin' Lion Farted! My people will choke under burdensome taxation to furnish this figurehead, rubber-stamping monarch with lavish palaces and castles and a lifestyle of obscene wealth, bejeweled crowns, ridiculous regal robes and silly uniforms, global travel, ribbon cutting, polo and tennis tournaments, and parading as a spoiled, entitled asshole. In contrast, the people sacrifice and suffer." He said repeatedly.

The people remained grateful to King Sean by contributing gratuities on his birthday, New Atlantica Day, which commemorated the open border immigration and public land grants by lottery, all legal and non-legal holidays, and any occasion they chose to pay tribute to the immensely popular Squire, King, and Benefactor.

"The king must be cajoled into abdication by promises of a comfortable retirement." The professor concluded. The public would never tolerate a violent coup. Any attempt to overthrow their king would create a mass revolt of vengeance. The only way the people turn against their adored monarch would be to manufacture evidence of reason, betrayal, malfeasance, or some unforgivable act of evil treachery, greed, or capital crime. Assassination would be met with reprisals. The triarchy might survive if blame could be diverted to some foreign power, insurrection by a subversive radical group, or retaliatory vengeance by the cartels. "Gillis was right. There must be a fall guy or a conspiracy. And Gillis and the Cartels were credible patsies."

The triarchy would then become a functional dualism with the professor as political head of the government, feeding Schvinghammer's massive ego by finally promoting him to Field Marshal in full command of a standing army and overall command of the militias.

There was one major problem with that solution: the professor and the general despised each other. The professor was an undeclared inveterate socialist, the general a strict Prussian militarist and nationalistic reactionary. The professor would be constantly looking over his shoulder or listening to the sounds of the night for military arrest like some despotic banana republic president, overthrown and possibly executed in a military coup. At the same time, the general—the Field Marshal—declared Martial Law like Trujillo, Marcos, or Pinochet.

He preferred not to work with Schvinghammer, who favored a military junta. The general would have to go!

Gunter-Ellis momentarily thought of accusing Schvinghammer and his military coup, tarnishing his reputation, discrediting him, and letting the masses choose some fitting punishment. "I could wash my hands of Schvinghammer like a modern-day Pontius Pilate." Suddenly, he realized what he had said to himself, the odious comparisons. "What am I thinking?" He uttered to himself, arguing with his brain. "The general is the furthest thing from Christ!" He caught his mind wandering into unfamiliar areas, plotting murders. He was no warrior. He was an academic! "Schvinghammer may have a Messiah complex, but he is not Jesus Christ, Mohammed, or Buddha," he shouted at the ceiling. Suddenly fearing the Wrath of God, Allah, Amun-Ra, Zeus, and every Supreme Being of every known religion past and present, the professor declared, "Schvinghammer is no messiah! He is merely afflicted with a messiah complex like Papa Doc Duvalier, Idi Amin, Hitler, and Napoleon Bonaparte."

Moving against the general would be far too dangerous given the fast-growing power of the provincial militias, his loyal volunteers, and professional mercenaries. The general had access to modern technology, sonar, satellites, drones, and a network of spies. The professor would need a mole, a spy, a fly on the wall, a traitor, or military rival, or a group of high-ranking military officers, possibly generals, admirals, and air marshals, to eliminate Schvinghammer the way Brutus, Cassius, and their knife-wielding senators slayed their dictator, Julius Caesar. "Et tu, Professor?" He chuckled.

The only remaining option would be an unexpected *natural* death or to quickly fabricate a conviction on some disturbed loner like Guiteau or Oswald.

A natural death, a heart attack, or stroke using an undetectable fatal injection would cripple the country, casting its populace into a long, inconsolable mourning period during which a new government would be installed without notice while the public grieved. When the mourners finally awakened from the funeral rites, the new republic would have already proclaimed, **"The king is dead. Long live the Republic."** The professor grinned. Amy Logan smiled at her husband with approval, bending over to kiss his forehead.

The Gathering Storm, Strike!

The Moles Go Underground.

The Isla de Granito de Ebano rock miners, derogatively labeled "moles" by the Triarchy and leading islanders, voted for the first time in their long mining colony history to strike for better wages, hours, working conditions, and healthcare. And to evade the strike-breaking thugs hired by Gillis and provided by the cartel, the miners and their families had gone underground.

The great, sleek, towering boulder, Isla de Granito, was unscalable and virtually unassailable. An impregnable fortress, drones, helicopters, and other rotary aircraft were surprised that the "worker bee" rock mining "moles" had secured and installed surface-to-air laser weaponry to protect the isle from airborne invasion. The strike could potentially continue so long as food, water, and other resources lasted. And, sympathetic supporters of the miners, probably the same group that incited the strike, were successful in night drops. The miners refused to negotiate. Now, they declared themselves a self-governing autonomous nation.

Xenophobia Among Generational Immigrants.

> "The life of a single human being is worth more than all the property of the richest man on earth."
>
> —Ernesto "Che" Guevara.

—

"Given space available, people have a right to live wherever they wish unless you're prepared to accept the irrationality of Geographic Pre-destination." Alexandre Begre' had lectured an anti-immigration group at a public hearing.

The xenophobia of the first generational immigrants was at best ironic, at worst hypocritical. They had been transported to New Atlantica primarily to the main island, a few distributed to the smaller perimeter islands and islets, and some scattered along the eastern outer banks as homeless, destitute people from around the globe, particularly impoverished third-world countries. Their Host, known at the time simply as Squire Sean (the Benefactor) working with the A.N. (Alliance of Nations) and worldwide secular and non-secular charities had assisted their settlement with multiple free services, house construction, potable water and nutritional food supplies, educational and vocational services, equitable land distribution, agricultural and industrial grants and interpreters and lessons to overcome the many language barriers between these new settlers. Scientific grants soon provided that fresh drinking water was in abundance through the crisscrossing canals. Filtration systems converted ocean saltwater to fresh drinking water. The water could then also be diverted for irrigation without saltwater damage to the soil and freely accessed for fire protection. Solar, water, and wind power provide clean energy for electricity.

But despite these blanket charitable gifts of conveniences, the first generation of settlers typically resented the succeeding groups of settlers with familiar prejudicial diatribes, "Go back to where you came from! They're stealing our jobs! There are too many people here already! You're ruining the environment! We don't want you here!" And the old standard lie, "We were here first!" No one was able to say, "I was born here" (invoking the flawed philosophical argument of geographic predestination) because none of them were. Yet the 1st generational immigrants never hesitated to shout obscenities, blaming the new arrivals for all their problems—because blaming others is always easier than brutal honesty and responsibility-and more than a few threatened the 2nd generation with bodily harm and even death. The previous scapegoats naturally sought out new targets to divert racial or cultural hatred away from themselves.

When Queen Malika labelled xenophobic blind hatred "witch burning," King Sean warned, "Burning witches is always bad karma."

The king remained optimistic that he could heal the animosity. Alexandre's "Mon ami, you cannot reason with unreasonable people." Alexandre told Sean and Malika.

The 2nd generation was not seeking conflict.

Still, they toured provinces, trusting that the king's popularity and personal appeals could mend rifts between the two groups. The new immigrants were not seeking conflict, the royal tried to explain, "Just new lands to settle."

"Yes, our land!" The 1st generation shouted. "Send them back wherever they came from! We don't want them here!"

"It is, in fact," Malika said loudly and firmly, correcting the crowd, "His Majesty's land, his island."

"Your Majesty," the king said, speaking quietly and respectfully to his queen. "I did grant most of the lands to the first wave." Turning back to the crowd, he then reminded them. "You were not here first. There were squatters, the Ybanis, explorers, aquatic animals, mammals, sea life in tide pools, crevices, and craters, and…the Aquarians."

Malika looked at him. "Are they not a myth?"

The king shook his head quietly murmuring, "No."

Someone from the crowd had overheard. "Those creatures, those beasts are extinct— if they ever existed, at all."

Another crowd member demanded, "How come no one's ever seen one?"

A believer yelled, "Have you ever seen oxygen?"

The king addressed the crowd again. "Aquarians did exist. They do exist. They've always existed before time. I have met the. I have talked to Aquarians. I have learned from them about living in peace with all things. They are mystical like the Ybani people, mystical, not mythical."

"There is more land. Not everyone needs to live on the coast or in the cities, like sardines in a can." He tried to reason with the angry first settlers. "There is enough to share with the *second wave* of immigration, fertile land in Central New Atlantica."

"There is no land there!" The crowd rumbled. "That land is all leased to the industries for starvation wages!"

"We'll find the land; we'll make land available." The king assured the crowd. "I am not going to turn homeless people away. I am not going to cast them back into the sea like pebbles and stones."

"There will be land available soon, Your Highness," Malika told him quietly, "as soon as that awful Gillis and his cartel mobsters are deported."

The king nodded. "That's right. We can set up campgrounds for the new immigrants on public land until we clear the cartels out of the central region." He said, without mentioning Gillis. The omission did not escape Malika's notice.

"We'll make this work, but there is going to have to be a lot less land greed! When it's gone, it's gone." The king lectured amid angry shouts, catcalls, whining, and rumbling.

Sean raised and waved his arms to quiet the crowd. As the shouting faded to a dull roar, the king unexpectedly launched into a scolding paternal lecture.

"This is not exclusively your land but our Shared Country, belonging to all of us. Then, the king delivered his sternest lecture ever to his quarreling people. "You cannot take back a country which you never owned! You can no longer claim exclusive ownership of this land and this soil than snails and slugs that dwell peacefully upon its crust—bequeathed to me through hereditary birth error to be bequeathed again by altruistic charity to the homeless, the heartbroken, the impoverished, the abused, the disillusioned, disappointed, displaced, despondent, disheveled, and the disinfected!

People can no longer choose the place of their birth than they can pre-determine their ancestry, parents, race, or gender. Unless you are prepared to argue the geographic pre-destination, you have no more claim to a piece of soil than anyone else. We are born where and when we are born because that is when and where our mothers went into labor! It is not a proprietary right nor an inherent privilege! If this nonsense doesn't stop, I'll evict every damn one of you! Make peace and learn to live together as a cooperative community!"

After concluding his speech to a quiet, humbled audience and grumbling almost inaudibly to Malika, "Sometimes I feel like a damn babysitter," the king and queen walked bravely through to the crowd, to an awaiting helicopter to depart to the next province.

Malika took his hand as the helicopter rose from the ground to comfort him. He trembled slightly, visibly upset.

"I shouldn't have spoken to them that way." He said quietly and sadly.

"My darling, you cannot always make your people happy." She said, gently.

"I thought I could." He lamented as the helicopter rose higher, flying to the next province.

Implicating Ridgeway.

"Before we can remove the king and abolish the monarchy," the professor told Schvinghammer and Gillis, "we must rid ourselves of Breck Ridgeway."

To that end, the triarchy developed plans to erode the foundation under the crusading prime minister.

Through bribery, blackmail and extortion tactics culminating in mob-like threats supposedly by the cartels and political pressure, Gunter-Ellis had maneuvered himself into the foreign ministry and his handpicked allies onto the weak provisional cabinet replacing those timid and frightened ministers who suddenly began sporadically resigning citing the usual transparent political excuses; to spend more time with the family, return to their private sector jobs, explore other opportunities or undisclosed health problems.

Without telling the king, Gunter-Ellis, having quietly assumed the duties and position of foreign minister, was now third in the line of succession directly behind the high-strung, bespectacled, and scrawny bookkeeper deputy prime minister, Sanford Quinlan, and the prime minister. The young, politically ambitious prime minister, Breck Ridgeway, campaigned through the provinces to shore up support for his permanent leadership, a constitutional convention, and a federal republic to replace the sputtering cabinet-style bureaucracy with himself at the helm.

Never afraid of launching stinging attacks on the incompetence of his immediate predecessors, Ridgeway steered clear of any criticism of the monarchy. The king remained immensely popular, although more so for his engaging friendliness, empathy, and compassion for the masses than for his governing skills. The king, he reasoned, was the most effective public relations personality, an irreplaceable symbol of unity among the diverse masses. The people loved him and would tolerate no personal ridicule or political attacks on the Great Benefactor. A forced abdication was out of the question. The people would never allow it! It would be wiser to ease him into a comfortable early retirement gradually, well-deserved and rightfully earned.

Prime Minister Ridgeway's oratory began reaching fever-pitch demagoguery. The news media and the politicos expressed alarm. Psychiatrists whispered of his exhibiting traits of narcissism, other bolder experts, mostly first-year psychology students, risked defamation suits invoking such reckless, premature diagnostic terms as a megalomaniac and a less libelous cult of personality.

But he had no such predilections concerning the former P.Ms. "Jack" Balfour and "Old

Buck" Cannon were both dead. Any slanderous defamation of character or personal abuse of the deceased represented a futile waste of time and energy. The dead don't care what is said of them. "Never speak ill of the dead, far better to speak of the living."

"Handsome Hank" Bryce vanished into political obscurity and irrelevance, his occasional editorial outbursts falling on deaf ears. His health continued to deteriorate from drug abuse.

Balfour, the chain-smoking, beer-guzzling, explosive and overweight Field Marshal, was a "heart attack and stroke waiting to happen," his doctors had for years warned him to no avail. The general believed himself invincible, stating that if direct combat failed to kill him, his unhealthy habits and diets could do no worse.

Cannon's resume as a diplomat was impressive. Much was expected of Cannon as a skilled diplomat and negotiator. But he was an inept administrator. Presidents and prime ministers had always formulated policies. It was his task to negotiate it with foreign leaders as their representative.

Occasionally, Ridgeway misread the fervor of the crowd and slipped into anti-monarchy demagoguery. The crowds went silent. The king remained immensely popular. Then, the embarrassed prime minister, trying to recover from a career-ending faux pas, suddenly realized that the rumblings of republicanism were a reactive condemnation of the weak cabinet-style bureaucracy rather than any sudden disaffection for the beloved king. There was no talk among the rank and file of overthrowing the king nor forcing his abdication, other than a well-deserved retirement at a time of the sovereign's choosing. Ridgeway would not again venture into political quicksand, but it would be weeks before the public, mass media, and social networks would forgive his miscalculated blunder.

After awaiting another serious gaffe, the triarchy eventually correctly concluded that the young prime minister was unlikely to commit political suicide with overzealous, fever-pitched demagoguery. They were neither willing to accept the continuation of the monarchy nor the timely formation of a republic under the charismatic leadership of the youthful Breck Ridgeway. A coup or assassination would assuredly backfire and render their regime operationally ineffective, illegitimate, and universally unpopular from the beginning—the inability to govern required alternate plans.

Resolving the Ridgeway Dilemma.

Selective historical research unfairly biases the honorable intention of the victors while ignoring the legitimate grievances of the defeated.

Gunter-Ellis, the professor, possessed an academically based knowledge of economic models. Schvinghammer, the general, thoroughly understood prudent military operating budgets. Whereas Gillis, the billionaire corporate raider and real estate tycoon, acquired working knowledge of economics through a practical seat-of-the-pants acumen. Although a retailer's quick pick machine randomly printed the multi-hundred-million-dollar ticket for him, Gillis, in a televised interview, discounted dumb luck. Instead, he reverted to his all-too-familiar swaggering *braggadocio* that his advanced, genius-level intellect had telepathically predetermined the winning numbers. However, he did avoid the foolishness and personal spendthrift irresponsibility of the mythical lottery curse that caused some individuals to mishandle their sudden unearned fortune, leading them into bankruptcy. Gillis immediately disowned his entire family, immediate and distant relatives alike, and renounced all friendships as well as casual acquaintances. The former ne'er-do-well wisely hired a reputable financial advisory team to invest his funds in a diversified strategy portfolio that consistently produced immense profits. Typically, Gillis self-promoted his public image as a shrewd investor without crediting his advisers. Quietly, collecting their fees and commissions, they allowed their billionaire client his instantaneous unmerited celebrity. The public was not fooled; Gillis remained unfazed by the scornful laughter and lack of idolatry.

The general and the tycoon, as devotees to laissez-faire economics, abhorred government intervention in economics; the socialist-leaning professor was a proponent. Schvinghammer and Gillis generally accepted that supply and demand trends impacted cyclical market fluctuations, prices rose whenever demand exceeded supply, falling when the desire for products, commodities, and services was low. The general only cared about securing adequate military supplies at favorable prices, purchasing in discounted bulk whenever possible with the off-the-book savings reallocated into untraceable offshore bank accounts.

The professor shared with his two collaborators that false narratives depicting recessions and expansions might manipulate the free market rather than patiently waiting for a short-term economic downturn to tarnish the credibility and public persona of Ridgeway. As calamitous events worsened, the professor predicted, the public outcry would demand that the king dismiss Ridgeway. However, it was unlikely, especially with Begre as First counselor, that the professor and general would themselves benefit, barring election.

"The king has the authority to call elections. A committee of influential citizens led by an unsuspecting Ridgeway might sway the king for a vote of no confidence." The professor further explained.

"And Ridgeway is so self-enamored," Amy Logan added with a slight smirk, that he will not even recognize that he is the sacrificial lamb."

Then, Gillis suggested a more scandalous tactic to chase the political upstart out of office, with Schvinghammer supplying the operatives and the cartels with the required funds. Gunter-Ellis could use his influential contacts, maneuvering the international news media to publish a far-reaching, damning exposé of the rising political star.

The professor dissented, reminding Gillis of plausible deniability, emphasizing that just the appearance of impropriety or culpability in any plot, conspiracy, or political intrigue would backfire, resulting in permanent ostracization to the political wilderness in perpetual exile alongside the disreputable, addicted failure "Handsome Hank" Bryce.

The general had remained quietly attentive throughout the discussion, only nodding occasionally when in agreement with the better suggestions. Finally, he stood to speak as if addressing the troops before a high-casualty invasion. They all turned to listen, half-expecting an introductory, "Some of you will not return from this mission."

"We shall cover our tracks and conclusively disavow any complicity or participation in any political plot, conspiracy, or coup. I have done this successfully many times in the past. As a military tactician, no prudent commander launches an offensive maneuver without considering alternate plans of attack, diversionary tactics, exit strategies, tactical withdrawals, and retreating defensive actions to regroup for a counterattack with the least humiliation, casualties, and loss of morale possible."

To the men's surprise, especially the general, Amy Logan nodded in support of the general. She raised her hand in support of the general.

"We achieve plausible deniability and cover our tracks, diverting suspicion away from us by attacking from simultaneous fronts and flanks. I vote in favor of the general's tactical proposal."

The professor and the tycoon made it unanimous in a voice vote, leaving Schvinghammer to his plans in strict privacy and report back to them at the next meeting, the time and location to be conveyed by coded message.

The Governors' Petition.

> "The government should help and guide the weak and small racial groups within its national boundaries toward self-determination and self-government."
>
> —Sun Yat-sen.

> "The best government is that which teaches us to govern ourselves."
>
> —Johann Wolfgang von Goethe.

The professor accompanied a delegation of provincial governors in his limited capacity as an unbiased adviser and indifferent observer. He insisted on delivering a petition to the informal, receptive king.

King Sean (Fidwitter), the "commoner king," received them cordially, greeting them each personally by first name from memory, thanking them for the visit, and bringing their concerns directly to him in his typically warm, well-mannered, and down-to-earth style. He was dressed casually in a denim shirt, blue jeans, and sandals, without a hint of pretentious royal extravagance. Then, without the assistance of domestic servants, he offered to serve refreshments before commencing the "official business" meeting.

"Oh, please, have a refreshment. I'm drinking—Ybani fruit juice Orange, today!" He encouraged them as they gathered at the refreshment table.

Borrowing the Round Table concept from Arthurian legend, he had personally arranged the comfortable, thick, cushioned, high-back chairs in a circle to avert any suggestion of hierarchy; no one was seated at the head or foot of any conference table. He had, several days before, declined a seating chart in favor of open seating, encouraging the governors to randomly choose any chair they liked, all of them identical and designed for comfort. The king waited until all were seated before occupying the remaining empty chair. But suddenly he jumped up, alarmed that Gunter-Ellis was standing alone outside the circle, in silent but stern observation and looking painfully dejected.

The professor quickly noticed that Queen Consort Malika Bello and First Counselor

Alexandre Begre were missing. He found it curious, as Sean seldom, if ever, conducted official or even unofficial government business without them. That they might join the conference later, unannounced, briefly occurred to him, but for the moment, he is entrapping his unsophisticated, naïve former student, the king.

Sean ran apologetically to the professor, guiding him back into the circle, politely offering his chair to the professor. Then, the king dashed out of the room, returning with a plain folding wooden chair and slid unobtrusively back into the circle.

"Governors, professor, please commence. You have my undivided attention."

The governors passed their petition to Sean, who began reading it at once, nodding and murmuring approvingly with each paragraph. As he finished reading the documents, a nervous governor spoke for the group.

"Your Majesty," he began.

Sean cut him off quickly but kindly with a dismissive arm motion.

"No, no, not 'your majesty.' We're not doing that today. I've never been comfortable with that. Let's keep this friendly and informal. Call me Sean."

The governors squirmed nervously, uncomfortable with Sean's informality.

"Okay," Sean relented, referring to his earlier days as the 'benefactor,' "then 'Squire,' but none of that unearned, undeserved loftiness. So, you want to form a parliament? That was always my intention. Do I need to sign this?"

"Your Highness," a governor addressed him, then quickly corrected himself as Sean shot him a stern look, "Squire, the prime minister told us that the King's Charter doesn't provide for a legislative body."

"Well then, we'll amend the charter," Sean said, casually. "Micromanaging bureaucrat," the king muttered aloud. "We'll amend that, too." Then, inaudibly beneath his breath, he grumbled, "I'll amend his ass."

The professor, looking alarmed, interrupted. "Your Excellency,"

"Excuse me?" Sean coughed and glared severely back.

"Squire," the professor corrected himself, though disapproving of the lack of protocol, "it is the consensus of the prime minister and cabinet that the people may not yet be ready to govern themselves."

"I dissent! I believe the people are more than ready." Sean responded, nodding and smiling at the governors. "I have complete confidence in their ability, their wisdom, and their sense of fairness. I thought they were ready on day one, but I was overruled by aristocratic elitist snobbery. Ah! Another amendment! The government, prime minister, and the cabinet offices shall no longer be appointed, but all public offices shall be elected by universal suffrage. Now, what should be the voting age, 15, 16, older, younger? He mused to the professor's horror. "What is the current acceptable age of maturity? I don't mind them voting, but we should discourage childhood pregnancies or the boys running off to war to kill or be killed by strangers rather than obnoxiously annoying their parents, teachers, and other adults. I believe that your new parliament should determine the voting age.

"How large a parliament do you propose, Squire?" A governor asked.

The king shrugged. "I shouldn't have to decide everything. Call the contractors, call the builders. How large of a building do you think you'll need?" He grinned to everyone's amusement, uncertain if he was jesting.

"I meant how many members, Sir?" The same governor smiled.

"As many as you want." Sean shrugged, writing notations on the petition. "It's none of my concern. I don't have a fish in this pond. "

An anxious Gunter-Ellis visibly bristled in his seat. This democratic republic government, sanctioned by the king, was feared to be premature.

"Surely this does not include the monarchy?" A supportive governor asked with alarm. The other governors nodded in unanimous agreement.

"You know," Sean mused aloud, "I never planned to keep this title for this long. It's had its moments of fun and pleasure, but the whole idea of a monarchy is rather silly and self-indulgent. My anti-monarchy rants are now a matter of public record, I hope. I am no hypocrite. How could such an outdated privilege be right for me if not right for everyone? It's not like I slew a dragon, pulled Excalibur out of a rock, or led an army of knights to victory in battle like Joan of Arc, or performed miraculous acts of valor. I was merely bequeathed an island, an island no one even knew was here for centuries until it surfaced from under the neglected doldrums, an island that existed long before any of us."

The governors shifted in their chairs uncomfortably. They looked at each other in disbelief. They, too, like their constituency, superficially represented, were exceedingly fond of their king. New Atlantica would not seem the same without Sean as their king, even as a symbolic, ceremonial figurehead.

The professor watched with interest and surprise. "Maybe they, the triarchy," he thought to himself," the combined militias under Schvinghammer, cartel hit squad, the Dons, influenced by Gillis, need not have to actively remove an immensely popular king from power and risk provoking a reactionary uprising. Could he, the professor, lacking the charisma of the king and the current prime minister, Breck Ridgeway, prevail in a popular election? Could the general be elected Defense Minister of a sedate, peaceful populace?"

"No, no Squire, please reconsider!" The governors rose to plead.

Sean waved them off, motioned them to return to their seats, again.

"I have always suspected," Sean smiled, only partly in jest, "that the Universe probably does not revolve around me, any one person, group, or nation, for that matter. The value of any opinion or point of view divided by the world population is minuscule, likely microscopic. Now, let us retire for dessert and indulge in ample slices of humble pie."

The governors began following their democratic king to the dessert table. The professor burst forward. "False Modesty! The man has lost his mind!" He raved silently, "I always suspected him insane! Now, I'm convinced!"

"Is our beloved king entertaining abdication?" The professor pleaded with blatant insincere flattery, shrewdly disguised. "Dare our benevolent squire-king cast us adrift in seas of anarchy and deny us his wise leadership?" He continued with overt, nearly Shakespearean dramatics. "I beg you, Sir, do not abdicate during such perilous times."

"Abdicate? Abdication has such severe connotations," he joked, sardonically, "France's childlike, idiotic king, Louis XVI, trying to outrun the guillotine, the German Kaiser unfairly indicted as a war criminal, the inept Russian Czar stupidly awaiting the arrival of the bloodthirsty Bolsheviks."

"In fairness, the Kaiser got away." The governor reminded everyone.

"And lived to a ripe old age, residing in a comfortable manor in Holland, chopping firewood." Recalled another amused governor.

"The czar and his family awaited execution, freezing in Siberia of all places!" A third governor joined the chortling history lesson.

"Yes, I think retirement sounds much safer, at the convenience of the parliament by request from the elected head of government, of course." He bowed slightly to the governors, then began serving the desserts to them.

The Recession Hoax:

"It's the economy, stupid."

—James Carvelle.

"It's the stupid fuckin' economy!"

—Jake Gillis.

Jake Gillis growled at the start of the meeting. Then, more calmly, he offered his plan to the others quickly assembled at the undisclosed remote location on the perimeter islets. "The idea is to have the people turn against the king, who won't know what to do, and Ridgeway, who should have known what to do but didn't."

"People facing starvation are seldom patient and understanding with delays in public assistance services. I predict they'll revolt." Gunter-Ellis noted.

"We know that abject poverty and severe hunger incite riots in the marketplace and foment revolution. But I have no desire to recruit an army of emaciated peasants too weak to fight and kill." Schvinghammer boomed.

"Capitalistic, free market economies have always oscillated in cyclical waves. The pendulum will swing back from negative growth contraction, eh recession," he simplified the terms, "to economic growth and business expansion as the upward cycle rebounds. The length of the recession's period is determined by either initiating government stimuli or subscribing to self-correcting laissez-faire economics over a longer period. It all depends upon your prevailing economic philosophies and the patience and degree of suffering an economic constituency is willing to endure." The professor lectured as his co-conspirators nodded impatiently.

"We can create a recession that won't correct itself until we rid the country of both the king and Ridgeway!" Gillis stated.

"I suppose we can create the conditions." Advised the professor.

Within days, Gillis announced worker lay-offs and industrial downsizing. The provincial government, taken by surprise, had no labor displacement or unemployment program. Quinlan, the bureaucrat, scrambled to resolve the situation by appealing directly to Gillis and all his associates, including the Cartel, to stave off economic austerity by keeping the factories open in full production. Gillis and the Cartel, both already under scrutiny by Cassie McGinnis and the Justice Ministry, went into lock-down mode without offering worker relocation, severance pay, or unemployment benefits. Gillis justified the lay-offs and shutdowns by insisting that over-production, exorbitant wage demands, and declining sales had forced the factory closures despite the widely held disclaimers by economic experts.

Gillis and the Cartel covertly continued production and shipping orders behind closed doors by importing scab labor and shipping orders under the cover of darkness.

The Cartels' downsizing was not a ruse as Cassie continued executing search and seizure orders and deporting its soldiers and minions with criminal records.

"That bitch has gotta go!" The Dons declared expanding their hit list to include the monarchy's inner circle of friends, closest associates, and loyal supporters, the King, Cassie McGinnis, and her team at the Justice Ministry, Alexandre Begre', Darissa, the Ybani ambassador, and Ybani Royal Guard, and even the Queen Consort, Malika Bello.

The Ridgeway Resolution

> "Power is always dangerous. Power attracts the worst and corrupts the best."
>
> —Edward Abbey.

> "It's not power that corrupts but the fear of losing it."
>
> —Bill Moyers.

"How soon we forget."

"Hank Bryce is dead." The deputy prime minister, Sanford Quinlan, announced.

The cabinet members rustled anxiously and impatiently in their chairs, grumbling disinterestedly among themselves.

"Who did he say died?" A minister asked.

"Did you say Bryce or Price?" Another minister called out.

"Bryce!" The secretary shouted.

"Bryce, Bryce… Frank or Hank?" Asked the general seated at the far end of the long conference table, huddled in whispers with the professor.

Gillis eyed them suspiciously from the other end of the table.

"Oh, Frank!" Shouted another voice.

"Franklin Rice?" An older, hearing-impaired minister asked over the table talk.

"That can't be right." Someone disputed.

Then, further annoying Quinlan and the recording secretary, someone else blurted out, "I don't recall any Franklin Rice in the cabinet or anywhere!"

"Was he a governor, did he possibly work at some lowly office in one of the provinces?" Asked another, looking at the governors seated in uncomfortable folding chairs along the back wall. They shifted in their chairs, impatiently tapping their feet, waiting for the meeting to begin, their spokesperson constantly folding, unfolding, rolling, and perusing their petition now bearing the notarized signature and official seal of the king.

Cassie McGinnis groaned loudly, exasperated, shook her head, leaned back in her chair, closed her eyes, and refused to engage in the confused ramblings.

"Handsome Hank, Hank Bryce, goddammit!" The secretary rose halfway, shouting. "The goddamn former prime minister! Dammit! Who appointed you idiots?"

Several stood and looked at each other, stunned. "The king." They shrugged.

The secretary sat down, his face buried in his hands, mumbling in disgust.

"Bryce. He was right before Cannon, wasn't he?"

"It had to be before Cannon. But after Iron Jack."

"Phyllis Morehead briefly, then Bryce. He spent a lot of time in Rehab."

"So, how did he die? Bryce, I mean. Overdose?"

"Yes, of course," Quinlan answered without emotion.

"Oh, for fuck's sake!" Gillis exploded, jumping to his feet. "Are you going to have a fuckin' goddamn meeting or fuckin' not? Fuck the goddamn dead cokehead!

"Mr. Gillis, I remind you," Quinlan addressed him hesitantly. "That as an investment adviser without portfolio to the Finance Minister," he stammered, "that you are seated at this table strictly as a courtesy. I would ask respectfully that you refrain from further use of profanity."

"Oh, fuck this shit!" Gillis shouted as he took his seat, belligerently.

Then, gaveling the meeting to order, Quinlan reminded the cabinet, "We have a full agenda.

The older hearing-impaired minister pondered aloud, "Now, that's three prime ministers dead. Has anyone spoken to Mrs. Morehead? Is she well?"

"Oh, shut the fuck up, ya dumb old bastard!" Gillis shouted.

Quinlan slammed the gavel down onto the table, looking down to avert Gillis' glare.

"If anyone wishes a moment of silence…" He asked.

"The fucker's dead. No one remembers him, no one knew him, no one gives a flying ass fuck! Forget the goddamn crackhead and move on!" Gillis screamed.

This time, the burly general rose, pointed at Gillis, and snapped his fingers. Gillis sat, turned his chair aside, and stared silently at the floor.

The Agenda.

"All right," Quinlan sighed, finally relaxed. "This meeting is called to order."

"Where's Ridgeway?" Schvinghammer demanded to know.

"I don't know." Quinlan stammered, clearly shaken, and feeling—and looking out of place, unfamiliar in a leadership role. "He's campaigning …out in the provinces…making a lot of lofty promises, trying to build a base…to rally support to win favor…with the king to appoint to a full six-year term of office as prime minister with sweeping legislative powers."

The triarchy stirred in their seats, Gunter-Ellis and Schvinghammer exchanging concerned looks with Gillis at the end of the table, and Cassie McGinnis eyeing all three of them.

"Ya know he's promisin' under a Ridgeway Administration all the public utilities, power, water, transportation, schools, and the damn public services gonna be provided fer free!" "Gillis thundered.

As the ministers mumbled, Gunter-Ellis smiled slightly and pensively.

Then, Quinlan recaptured everyone's attention with a forced cough and gentle tap of the gavel on the table.

"In his absence, right now, I'm in charge here." Quinlan droned in his flat and tedious monotone voice as the ministers in unison groaned, "Oh gawd!"

"Roll call?" The secretary proctored Quinlan, trying to rescue him.

"We're all here." Quinlan snapped, looking around the table.

"Guests?" Asked the persistent secretary.

"The governors!" Quinlan sputtered with escalating annoyance. "They've been seated against the back wall the entire time!"

"Secretary's Report, minutes of previous meeting!" The secretary rose, speaking loudly.

Gunter-Ellis nodded to an ally who quickly rose, interrupting the secretary.

"I move we accept the minutes as written, waive the treasurer's report until next meeting, dispense with old business, and go directly to Item One under New Business Agenda."

"Second!" An unidentified voice rose, sounding like Gillis.

Before Quinlan could react, the general was on his feet, taking control of the meeting like a coup.

"All in favor? The ayes have it. Motion passed." The general declared boisterously, sitting down again, victoriously.

"I believe that Prime Minister Ridgeway is the agenda item." Gunter-Ellis smugly observed.

Quinlan, dazed and befuddled, asked meekly for the official report on "irregularities in the prime minister's accounts," followed by suspicious activities, withdrawals, and deposits in his personal bank accounts and stock portfolios delivered by somber-looking, impersonal, and frigid accountants and colorless, impassive bookkeepers.

Cassie McGinnis and several serious-looking Ridgeway loyalists thought the report was too packaged and neat, especially considering the prime minister's absence, thereby unable to deny or refute the charges. They feared that by the time he learned of it, additional charges and "false evidence" might be easily manufactured. She was anxious to examine the incriminating "irregularities" in Ridgeway's budget as well as the inflated deposits and expenditures in his bank statements, surmising the records had been doctored to create a convenient fall guy and remove their last remaining roadblock on the Triarchy's path to power.

Indictment.

"How quickly will Ridgeway be indicted?" The general bellowed at Cassie. "Do you need help with the arrest? Some of Gen II

(Second Generation immigrants who tended to be less loyal or severely hostile to the monarchy) may try to disrupt his arrest by chaining themselves together like those crazy tree huggers. I can order a preventive surgical strike to take them out."

"We are not proceeding on anything, General, until independent examiners have authenticated these invoices and banking records. I want to review the evidence personally. I am not convinced that this isn't a frame-up."

"Captain!" Schvingheimer grumbled in a barely audible voice.

"Colonel." She retorted sternly, her stance leaning toward him, her clenched fists pressed down upon the table. "I resigned my army commission as a colonel, fully vested retirement pays and benefits." She taunted him. "You may now and in the future please address me as Minister, Justice Minister.

"Begre'! Double-talking shyster lawyer!" The general groused, scornfully.

Quinlan, sensing tension, dissension, and flared tempers, glanced around the room nervously and suddenly declared the meeting adjourned.

The secretary tried to advise him of the procedure. Quinlan ignored him. The governors objected, one standing, waving the petition, trying to be heard above the angry voices and chair legs scratching the hardwood floor.

Quinlan perfunctorily dismissed them, stepping to them before dashing from the room. "Governors, I have reviewed an advance copy of your petition. The full cabinet reading of your petition must be tabled for three months!"

"Sanford fuckin' Quinlan, goddamn Acting Prime Minister!" Gillis was heard grumbling as the ministers left the building, ignoring him and fleeing him quickly. "Atrocious goddamn speller! He can't golf for shit. He slices the ball off the fuckin' fairway every-goddamn-time! Ya know he once beaned a dumbass groundskeeper a half mile away, sent him straight to the ICU!"

"You know that slimy worm Quinlan is not just going to surrender power to us." The general said quietly to the professor at the conference table once the others had all departed from the room. "After that sickly runt of the litter has sampled a taste of authority, the sniveling little office clerk will clutch onto power as tightly as anyone, he'll be like a blood-sucking leech on a bare leg in filthy, snake river infested water."

The professor nodded. "We can eliminate the minor actors from the play once they have delivered their throw-away lines, General. We will first write the stage directions for the principal actors to exit the scene. Then we can pull the curtain." The professor stated in coded theatrical metaphors, aware that the room might be "bugged" with hidden listening devices.

Then, as the custodians entered, they both paused dramatically from the unscripted dialogue and exited separately.

Sounding the Alarm.

Justice Minister Cassandra McGinnis and her former defense attorneys, First Counselor Alexandre Begre' and Queen Consort Malika Bello, had long suspected a coup in the planning stages or worse. The Ybanis had warned the king that a torrential island storm was brewing in the wake of the dynamic, fast-rising political star, the young, appealing, charismatic, and political firestorm Breck Ridgeway.

It was apparent to even the casual observer that the Triarchy would be seeking undue influence and control over the formation of any new government. They could not prevail in an open and general election, the professor too cold and elitist, the general too pompous and stern, and the bullying Gillis, crude and corrupt. Gunter-Ellis, without a germ of modesty, easily saw himself as the most eminently qualified to lead, indeed, to rule and govern the new republic. He might begrudgingly accept others into a bureaucratic plutocracy as technocrats, but he did not need nor wish their advice. They represented "excess baggage" to the professor. He would, at best, tolerate them in the same way that most politicians and bureaucrats conduct public hearings, by "nodding my head a lot while pretending to take notes."

"The economy will likely self-correct within a matter of a few months. In the meantime, my advice is to reduce your expenditures and eat less." Acting Prime Minister Sanford Quinlan stated, trying to reassure a struggling populace in a poorly received public policy statement. The economists argued in favor of Keynesian spending to stimulate the stalled economy. But Quinlan reaffirmed the program of austerity and introduced taxes to replace the dwindling national lottery.

Breck Ridgeway rushed back to Capitol City from the provinces, suspending his quixotic campaign to form a Republic under his leadership. Bursting into the office, he physically ejected Quinlan from his desk chair. When Quinlan protested that Ridgeway was "on unpaid administrative leave," the prime minister shoved his deputy P.M. out of the office and into the hallway, locking the door behind him.

Quinlan held a subsequent press conference in which he accused Ridgeway of illegally usurping his authority and demanded his arrest either by the Justice Ministry or by the military under martial law. The cabinet was equally divided on the rift and called upon the sovereign to settle the matter—the king, claiming it to be a legal dispute, deferred to First Counselor Beqre. The worldwide news media quickly picked up the story, and condescending political pundits, none of whom had ever sought elective office, watched with anticipation as the rift unfolded into a grave.

To avert a constitutional crisis, Begre' tried to intervene, but the two quarreling prime ministers refused to recognize his authority. Reporting back to the sovereign, the king wearily instructed his First Counselor to "fire them both" and assume the reins of power.

Begre' vehemently refused the demotion. "Am I never to leave this god forsaken island?" He protested.

With the king's notarized signature and royal seal embossed on the legal orders and armed guards for security, Begre soon returned to escort Quinlan and Ridgeway off the premises, placing both onto unpaid administrative leave, thus forcing them to seek gainful and more respectable full employment.

Gunter-Ellis, next in line of succession, became acting prime minister while still retaining the foreign ministry. The king was in check and in peril.

Your Queen Is In Danger!

"International diplomacy and international relations …(is) not a game of chess where two people sit quietly in a room and think about the moves they're going to make and take time between their moves."

—Madeleine Albright.

"One would think that people living among the beauty of Nature, anywhere, anytime, would not be so consumed in anger and hatred. Perhaps people as a species are more comfortable with conflict than peace."

—Sean I (Fidwitter).

In a desperate conspiratorial ploy, Jake Gillis had spread a false rumor that

Princess Lucia, the "distant cousin" of King Sean, the iconic "Greek goddess-like" wife of First Counselor Alexandre Begre' and mother of the 12-year-old crown prince, Pete Begre, was an alien being, perhaps a humanoid or hominid-like cryptid.

Finally, Gillis took the matter of the public demand that the Justice Minister order.

Princess Lucia submits to DNA & blood tests to verify her royal lineage. As expected, she declined with scornful laughter, suggesting that Gillis was "playacting the fool." Cassie McGinnis also refused to act, citing an apparent "want of jurisdiction in this silly matter."

The usually unflappable Alexandre Begre, in a rare fit of anger, located Gillis at a local neighborhood tavern, pulled him outside into the street, and challenged him to a fistfight in the middle of the street. Princess Lucia arrived shortly and stepped between them, halting their "pissing contest."

Begre' swallowed his pride and then returned home with his wife. Gillis loudly and boastfully claimed victory, even by default. He had no idea that most of the barflies had placed their bets favoring Begre.

Still, Cassie McGinnis agreed to Begre's request for inconspicuous, plain-clothed, unobtrusive armed guards to protect Princess Lucia and Crown Prince Pete from any perceived threats of harassment or physical harm.

The Ambassador.

"The roads to fame and glory are paved with pyrite."

-Author.

Cassie stepped briskly along the pyrite-plated walkway to the modest royal residence, reminded by the glitter of "fool's gold" of one of Sean's many offhand, facetious remarks, "The roads to fame and glory are paved with pyrite." She paused there for a moment, reflecting on the sovereign's frequent, self-deprecating jabs at all things royal, notably its supposed birthright to rule anything or anyone, hereditary wealth, and privilege at the expense of the over-burdened hardworking wage earners, entitlements pretensions and delusions of grandeur, a title he would have denounced had he not viewed his monikers of Sean the Benefactor and The Commoner King as an altruistic call to arms for the betterment of the world's most desperate refugees from chronic homelessness and heartless destitution.

She began again at a hurried pace, then stopped again, reverently waiting as the statuesque, bronze-skinned, stunning goddess-like Ybani Ambassador emerged through the arched doorway and approached her on the walkway.

Cassie stepped aside humbly and bowed slightly as if in the sudden, unanticipated presence of a European sovereign or an Asian emperor. The ambassador smiled kindly, waving off the gesture of reverent protocol.

The bronze-skinned, statuesque ambassador was in her early sixties.

Cassie rose, standing erect, nearly stumbling as the ambassador took her hand and gently pulled her back onto the walkway. "I know your king has dispensed with all the pomp and circumstance silliness, and he is your king. I am only an ambassador, a glorified messenger, a go-between. Do not make so much of me, Dear."

Then, pleasantly reminding Cassie, "Your king is waiting to speak with you," the ambassador turned and walked briskly down the walkway, disappearing into the evening fog.

A Royal Tour.

"You are escorting the Queen …on a global goodwill tour," Sean told his Justice Minister, Cassandra McGinnis, as they stood in the living room, his back to her as he gazed sadly out the bay window.

She noted that Sean as he preferred to be called, regardless of protocol, never used the word consort when speaking of his queen. Malika was always *"the Queen"* respectfully and affectionately.

Cassie was concerned by the unusually serious and worried look upon the face of the normally gregarious, fun-loving, and carefree king.

"Me? Your Highness, I am pursuing several criminal prosecutions. We're seeking multiple indictments as we speak." Cassie reminded him.

"There are others who can do this for you. This tour takes priority." The king told her calmly but firmly. "You both need to leave the island at once."

"Your Highness, I would prefer you send someone else." She politely demurred.

"How long will this royal tour be?"

"We have diplomatic visas. How long is this grand tour?"

"Until you are contacted that it's safe to return." The king told her in a quiet, somber voice and a sad, worried look upon his tired, haggard face.

Cassie was worried about Sean. He had aged terribly during the past three years. During the past year, the normally gregarious, extroverted king was reclusive, seldom leaving the residence, living like a hermit.

"Your Majesty, have you heard something?"

"Someone has." He mumbled knowingly.

"When do we leave?" She asked.

"Yesterday would be perfect." He answered solemnly.

Then, turning without further comment, he disappeared into his office.

"What has happened?" The Queen asked Cassie upon entering the room.

"We're embarking on a royal tour of the continents," Cassie answered quietly.

"When?" The queen asked curiously.

"As soon as you're packed,"

The Blockade.

A month later, with his queen and justice minister ensconced on a continental royal tour, the king awakened to the alarming sight of a naval blockade of Isla de Granito de Ebano.

"Is this necessary?" The king demanded, staring out the bay window at a fleet of battleships.

"It's only a blockade," Schvinghammer explained. "It's not an invasion."

"How is a labor dispute a matter for the military?" Alexandre Begre', stepping out of a darkened corner, challenged the general. Gunter-Ellis, the foreign minister and acting premier, Gunter-Ellis and his attractive, blonde wife, 28-year-old Amy Logan, joined them in front of the large bay window of the king's living room overlooking the Darwin Straits.

"We are not actively engaging the moles with boots on the ground." The general explained, annoyed and impatient. "We're just quashing an illegal strike."

"Who determined a labor strike to be illegal?" Begre demanded.

"Strategy II is to flush them out with unmanned air tankers." The general bellowed, talking over the lawyer. "Then, as the water floods into the mine shafts and escape tunnels, we'll drown them like the gophers, rats, and slugs that they are! We're going to flush the gophers out of their tunnels."

"That's inhumane!" The king shouted.

"And a clear violation of international law." Begre' added, stepping out of the shadows to the surprise of Schvinghammer.

"Then how would His Majesty and his First Counselor propose that we break this unlawful strike?" Demanded Gunter-Ellis joining the discussion.

"In what way is it illegal?" Begre' repeated, challenged the professor.

"By Mr. Gillis' lease agreement with the trustees." The professor countered. "The lease prohibits any work disruptions, slowdowns, strikes!"

"Those terms are unenforceable by international labor law." Begre' stated with assurance.

The professor eyed him, questioning, wondering if the lawyer was bluffing. Then, stammering, he countered, "I am not at all sure that international labor law applies to penal colonies and work camps."

"Jake Gillis claims it's not a prison camp!" The king interrupted.

"I think that is a matter for arbitration." The professor retorted.

"And in the interim, the naval blockade and aerial reconnaissance continue." The general growled, puffing out his bemedaled chest.

The king stepped forward, gesturing out the window. "Fuck no! That island out there, that miserable fuckin' penal colony, that massive black boulder of granite, the pile of rock belongs to me! It's part of my settlement! I own the goddamn archipelago! I'll just break the goddamn lease."

"No." Begre' quietly counseled him. "Gillis' lawyers would tie you up in litigation for years. Let the lease expire with no renewal."

Then, the weary, emaciated king, his face discolored from jaundice, his tooth-bitten lower lip trembling with soreness, and his eyes red from worried sleepiness, turned on his heels, nearly losing his balance, to confront the general eyeball-to-eyeball. The general startled, stepped back, accustomed to intimidating everyone around him—except the boldly aggressive, ever-confident litigator Alexandre Begre'.

"Explain the goddamn fuckin' navy, you pompous Prussian Martinet!" the King demanded, unusually confrontational.

"Why you little prick!" The general thundered.

Begre stepped forward, alarmed to protect the frail, sickly monarch. The professor, in shock, held back, his jaw dropping, his face ashen.

"General." Amy Logan cautioned, suddenly jumping into the fray from a darkened corner, placing herself between Schvinghammer and Sean.

"General! You are addressing the King!" She reminded him, trying to de-escalate the fiery confrontation.

"Stand down!" Sean calmly ordered the general. Then, Schvinghammer, flustered, retreated.

Gunter-Ellis immediately assumed a diplomatic pose. "Your Majesty," the acting prime minister and foreign minister bowed, speaking softly, "The naval ships are on loan from friendly and neutral nations. They are here only as a buffer to maintain order as a peacekeeping presence. They do claim a national interest but have agreed not to interfere with the labor negotiations." Pausing for the tension to subside, he asked, "How would His Majesty wish to proceed at this point?"

Begre' with the king's assent interjected, "Why not accede to their demands?"

"Unthinkable, Sir." The professor countered the proposal.

Amy watched in silent curiosity. But the red-faced general muttered angrily.

"If you give those people even a taste of freedom," grumbled the general, "and they'll demand more! Between those moles and gophers and your homeless, immigrant masses, we'll all soon be replaced by plebian mongrels! We'll become a minority!"

"General." Cautioned the professor Amy, and she cringed uncomfortably.

Amy Logan, the social-climbing former debutante eager for membership into the haut monde, had no love lost for the masses, but she was protective of the professor's political image. It would not denigrate the working class, especially in front of witnesses and possibly hidden listening devices.

"Why not just give them what they want?" The king pondered. "What harm can come from a healthier work environment and higher wages?"

"The commoner king." The general scowled under his breath.

The king continued, unimpeded. "Do we want a discontented labor force? They've toiled and lived under atrocious conditions for years. Give them their dignity, grant them autonomy."

"Pandora's Box, Your Highness." The professor cautioned. "If we lose Isla de

Granito de Ebano by granting them self-governing autonomy, the island provinces will secede as independent States and Republics. They will all fall like dominoes!"

"And there goes your empire!" the general roared.

"It's not an empire." The king admonished the general.

The king and Begre' then retreated to a corner to confer privately in whispers, and the professor and general sensed correctly that the meeting had concluded. The king and his counselor returned to dismiss them officially.

Thus, the professor turned abruptly to leave, followed by Amy, who paused long enough to curtsy to the king first with a flirtatious smile. Then, the general clicked his heels, saluted the king, turned, and followed them out of the residence.

As the general left the residence, he strutted past several young sentries, their erect muscular bodies standing stiffly with their cold eyes alert on the front porch. Each snapped sharply to full attention as the general, their arms raised to salute. He pivoted sharply, clicking his heels together, frowning at the first sentry, his brows furrowed, glowering sternly.

"Who posted you here?" the general growled.

"Sir, we are the king's royal guard."

"Do you know who I am?" Schvinghammer barked.

"Yes, Sir, General!" The sentry answered smartly and crisply. "You are General Eric von Schvinghammer, Defense Minister!"

"Then you are under my direct command to obey my orders without question!"

"Begging the General's pardon," the sentry replied, "we are the Royal Guard, Sir! Our singular duty is to protect His Majesty, the King. Our sworn allegiance is to His Majesty, the King. We obey only the orders of the King."

Schvinghammer turned sharply, pivoting on his heels. Then, marching briskly as in cadence down the walkway, muttering angrily to himself, "We will soon see about that!"

The Tunnel Rats.

The rock miners and their families dug deeper, creating an expansive hollowed shell out of the boulder-like island. They would not be flushed out or drowned, no matter how many destructive tons of seawater were dumped upon them from the air tankers. They burrowed deeper. The seawater, instead of flooding the underground communities, cascades out of all four black walls of the island through its darkened, hidden vents.

Schvinghammer, as Defense Minister, in desperation, ordered incendiary night bombings by the air corps. But even the mercenary pilots and crews refused on humanitarian grounds.

"The civilians are collateral damage. Their losses are inconsequential." The general told the suddenly moralistic professor and Amy Logan.

"We don't count children, their mommies, and the old people in the labor force. They are non-essential. If they should happen to drown, that's too bad. They shouldn't have been down in the tunnels." Gillis added, coldly, to Amy's anguish. The professor tried to comfort her, but she did not respond to either the general or the tycoon.

"You'll be surprised how quickly this strike crumbles once we threaten a striker's family." Don Anderson smiled, having used this threat many times. "They stop playing the brave, defiant hero the minute we put a gun to the head or a knife to the throat of a loved one." One of the capos laughed.

The Miners, though having anticipated a military or police invasion for over a decade, had enhanced their engineering skills by constructing a contour of underground escape routes dotted *with subterranean hamlets, villages, and* communities.

Small birdlike holes had been drilled along the exterior walls above the waterline to provide ventilation at every descending level.

The flood waters dropped from the sky onto the black boulder, cascading like a series of waterfalls into a system of canals before flowing out through hidden vents lining the outer walls of Isla de Granito de Ebano and back into the sea. Rock ceilings protected each level with escape hatches located at various points along the solid granite "floors."

At the north end of the island, slightly above sea level, the island's population could be loaded aboard the rescue ships provided by Greenpeace, Amnesty International, and other humanitarian non-profit organizations.

The flushing strategy failed to break the strike through mass drownings.

Lithium Deposits.

"Sooner or later, we will have to recognize
that the Earth has rights, too, to live
without pollution. What mankind must know
is that human beings cannot live without
Mother Earth, but the planet can live
without humans."

—Evo Morales.

"Together we shall save our planet, or
together we shall perish in its flames."

—John F. Kennedy.

Jake Gillis had been conspicuously absent
from the morning meeting with the king and
his first counselor to discuss the strike-
breaking blockade of Isla de Granito de
Ebano, the rock boulder mining colony. But
later, that evening, the professor, Foreign
Minister, and Acting Prime Minister Gunter-
Ellis, his 28-year-old wife Amy Logan, and
Defense Minister General Schvinghammer
reported to the "self-made tycoon" at his
seaside "cottage." As usual, his business
managers, the dons, and those cartel
capos who had not yet been deported were
also invited to the conference. The main
agenda item, once more, was the final
strategic disposition of the king and his
immediate royal coterie, the Queen, First
Counselor Alexandre Begre, Princess Lucia,
the 12-year-old Crown Prince Pete Begre',
Justice Minister Cassandra McGinnis and
staff members. The Ybani ambassador and the

royal sentries were included as possible collateral damage.

The Dons entered through a hidden, thatch covered rear doorway in disguise under the cover of darkness. Amy sat on the arm of the overstuffed chair with the professor, her fingers massaging his stiff neck. The other men, as always resentful her presence at this sausage fest, glared contemptuously at her, groaned loudly in exasperation at her many opinionated interruptions.

The professor leaned forward to report the king's "outrageous plans" to grant autonomy to the mining colony and his cavalier attitude provincial secession.

"This is going to seriously curtail your granite mining." The professor warned.

"We stopped mining granite and extracting graphite long ago when we retooled for more lucrative minerals and ores. The diamonds on Isla de Granito have been mostly depleted. We're mining them in space, now. If it ever leaks out just how much we're brought down here, diamonds won't be worth shit."

"But you're still mining nickel on that black boulder?" Don Anderson queried.

"Only as a ruse." Gillis scoffed. "The return on lithium is much better. But with the moles on strike and the king refusing to act tough…"

"You're mining lithium?" Amy Logan recoiled in shock. "Do you know what that does to the environment? You are destroying the very land you are trying to steal!"

"What are you, a tree hugger?" The general grumbled.

"Throw that bitch out of here!" Gillis yelled, losing his temper, menacingly eyeing her. The Dons' burly soldiers grabbed Amy roughly And dragged her kicking, punching, and screaming from the cottage. The professor watched helplessly and silently without a word of protest.

"The king," said the professor in a trembling, cracked, subdued voice, "will never permit the mining of lithium."

"Then, it's time for a more permanent solution," Gillis said to the Dons.

"You'll make a martyr out of him." The professor warned.

"There are ways of suppressing that, too." Spoke the general with quiet affirmation. "Perhaps, the king will simply disappear."

The Dons nodded at their capos and sergeants. The general and Gillis glanced at the Dons.

"I can conscript a few privates." The general offered.

"Moles," Gillis answered. "We'll use moles."

"Or so it must appear." One of the Dons said among the whispers.

Again, the professor said nothing.

Legacy.

> **"First do no harm"** (Latin: **Primum non nocere**).
>
> —**Hippocrates.**

"The measure of a man is what he does with power."

—Plato.

"Everyone sees what you appear to be; Few experience what you really are."

—Niccolò Machiavelli.

"You must leave this leave the island by tomorrow, no later." Sean told his best friend and adviser, Alexandre Begre'.

"Yes, I know, Mon Ami to Stockholm to petition for peacekeeping forces to secure the main island and mediate the strike on Isla de Granito de Ebano."

"Then, finally to resume your law practice. You are not returning to New Atlantica. It is no longer safe for you here." The king told him in sadness.

The king appeared to be in turmoil, clearly fearful and anxious. In all their years of friendship, since their first days in college, Alexandre Begre' had never seen him, the former bon vivant Sean Fitter, looking so worried, tired, and somber. Clearly, he was distressed and ill. Sweat beaded his forehead; his hands were clammy and cold and his eyes tire and yellow with jaundice. He trembled from body chills, dehydrated, and malnourished, he was thin and gaunt from nervous sleeplessness.

"I'll arrange for a pilot and crew for your flight." The king added as an afterthought. "You may spend tonight with your family and depart by noon, tomorrow."

"I am a pilot with my own private jet." Begre' reminded his worried friend.

"The princess can co-pilot and navigate. We'll dispense with the crew and the staff, take you and Pete into exile. Your queen was in danger. We had to sacrifice a Ybani bishop so we castle."

"I remain here." The king spoke quietly. "This island is my Legacy. This is where you took me to an uninhabited, unknown island to the doldrums, the court-ordered settlement of my illegitimate, absentee, dead beat father. It's all about destiny, now." Sean continued as Alexandre stared blankly and silently, stunned and awed by Sean's sudden wisdom and atypical eloquence. My legacy if I have one, my destiny for what it's worth is that of the commoner king, Squire Sean the Benefactor, a mere footnote in brief history of uncharted, undiscovered land mass in the dreadful Atlantic doldrums. This is the sanctuary, the safe harbor for the desperate, the destitute, the dejected and rejected, the invisible, homeless, unwanted, the great unwashed. This one act of compassion and the love of my queen is my redemption and my salvation as a reprobate."

"You are no reprobate. You are a wise and noble philosopher king. Votre Majeste' (Your Majesty) Mon Roi (my king)," Begre' uttered, in surprise," I fear we have all under-estimated, underrated and berated you."

"That goes without saying." The king smiled with slight embarrassment. "Au Revoir."

"Au Revoir, Mon Ami, until we meet again."

"We shall see." The forlorn king sadly bade his only faithful friend farewell.

"This Nation, indeed, this planet, will not be destroyed by weapons of mass destruction nor senseless war or toxic pollution, climate change, and soil erosion but by the irrational hatred in human hearts." King Sean I.

The Destinies: The Princess and the Crown Prince.

"What you leave behind is not what is engraved in stone monuments, but what is woven into the lives of others."

—Pericles.

"If you're going to live, leave a legacy. Make a mark on the world that can't be erased."

—Maya Angelou.

Alexandre Begre traveled alone to Stockholm without his family. Both his longtime best friend, Sean, and his wife of thirteen happy and romantic years, the princess Lucia, strenuously urged him not to return anytime in the foreseeable future. New Atlantica was no longer safe for the king or any of his entourage. There were treacherous, murderous enemies in every political camp, "I have planned for the protection and education of our son, simply named Pete, with the Ybanis, crown prince and heir apparent to the throne of his cousin and godfather, King Sean I.

As Begre' loaded the last of his luggage onto his private jet, he sadly reflected on the events of the previous evening.

"Our son and I cannot leave New Atlantica. Our destiny lies here. But you must go." The princess told him in the early morning hours, after several hours of torrid passion, for their final night together. "Your destiny is to return to your first love, the law, international law, that is your true passion."

"I will not leave here without you and Pete." He vigorously protested.

"You must! You have no right to alter our destinies." She said in quiet defiance. "It is Pete's destiny to govern as Crown Prince."

"Pete is still a boy, twelve years of age." Begre' argued.

"In growth, wisdom, and maturity, he is a man already. Chronologically, he is twelve. "The Ybanis will protect, cloister, and tutor for a decade and a half, one decade. Then his true destiny begins. If you interrupt, intercede, and alter the path of destiny, you cause all to suffer. She insisted.

"And what is your destiny?" He asked the princess.

"My destiny has already been fulfilled."

"I have the jet fueled, serviced, and ready to fly. Let me take you home."

"I'm home," she said. "This is home. It has always been my home," she added. Then she kissed him deeply and passionately, holding him tightly. "Go now. Go live your destiny, my husband," she whispered.

He knew that the princess and Pete could live safely with the Ybanis. Begre planned to return to the island once the time was right and the revolution was over. He had to go to Stockholm to save the king, his family, and the republic from a corrupt coup.

Checkmate!

"Most of wars or military coups or invasions are done in the name of democracy against democracy."

—Eduardo Galeano.

"The only way to deal with an unfree world is to become so absolutely free that your very existence is an act of rebellion."

—Albert Camus

At 1 p.m. London time, the BBC reported that a private jet piloted by Alexandre Begre, New Atlantica's Royal First Counselor, exploded over the North Atlantic near Irish airspace. The plane, which was headed to Stockholm for an emergency session of the Alliance of Nations' Peacekeeping Task Force, had no crew aboard. It remains unclear whether Princess Lucia de la Mer and her son, Crown Prince Pete, traveled with the renowned attorney.

That afternoon, by the Ybani forest, Princess Lucia said goodbye to her 12-year-old son, Pete, the Crown Prince of New Atlantica. After entrusting him to the care of the Ybani people, she then leapt from the edge of the northernmost peak of

New Atlantica, spiraling down into the treacherous currents and rocky waters of the Darwin Straits. Once safely underwater, she reversed her human metamorphosis and entered the underwater caverns of New Atlantica.

A dense fog enveloped the main island, located a few miles away. Sean Fidwitter, formerly of Northern Ireland, stood looking out the bay window of his modest residence. Armed individuals, disguised as Isla de Granito mine workers in full combat attire, swiftly moved across the front lawn. Soon, the sentries lay bleeding, enabling the guerrillas to invade the residence.

Returning to Capitol City, the interim prime minister turned to his wife, Amy Logan, and smiled, "The King is Dead. Long Live the Republic."

END